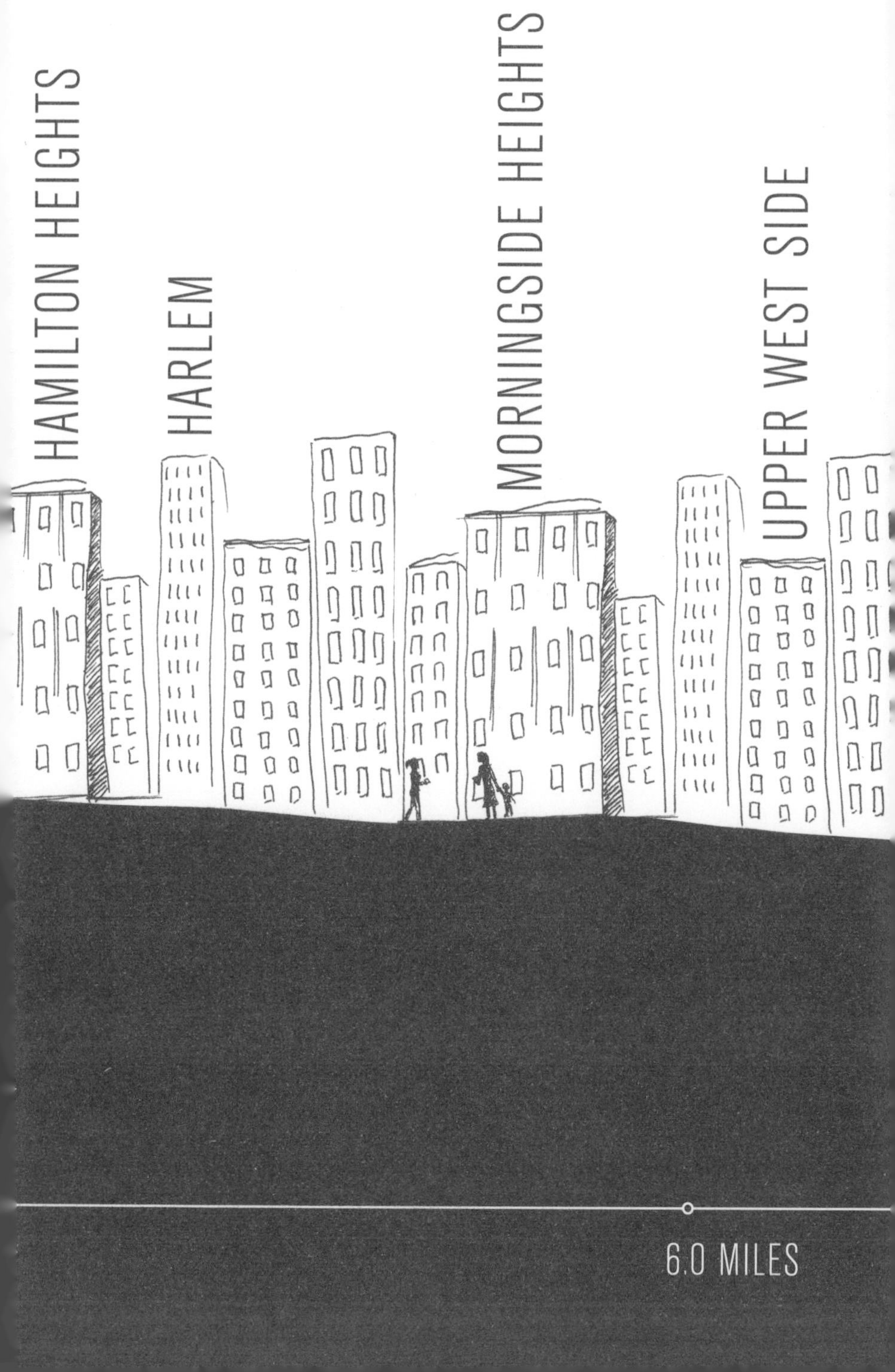

HAMILTON HEIGHTS

HARLEM

MORNINGSIDE HEIGHTS

UPPER WEST SIDE

6.0 MILES

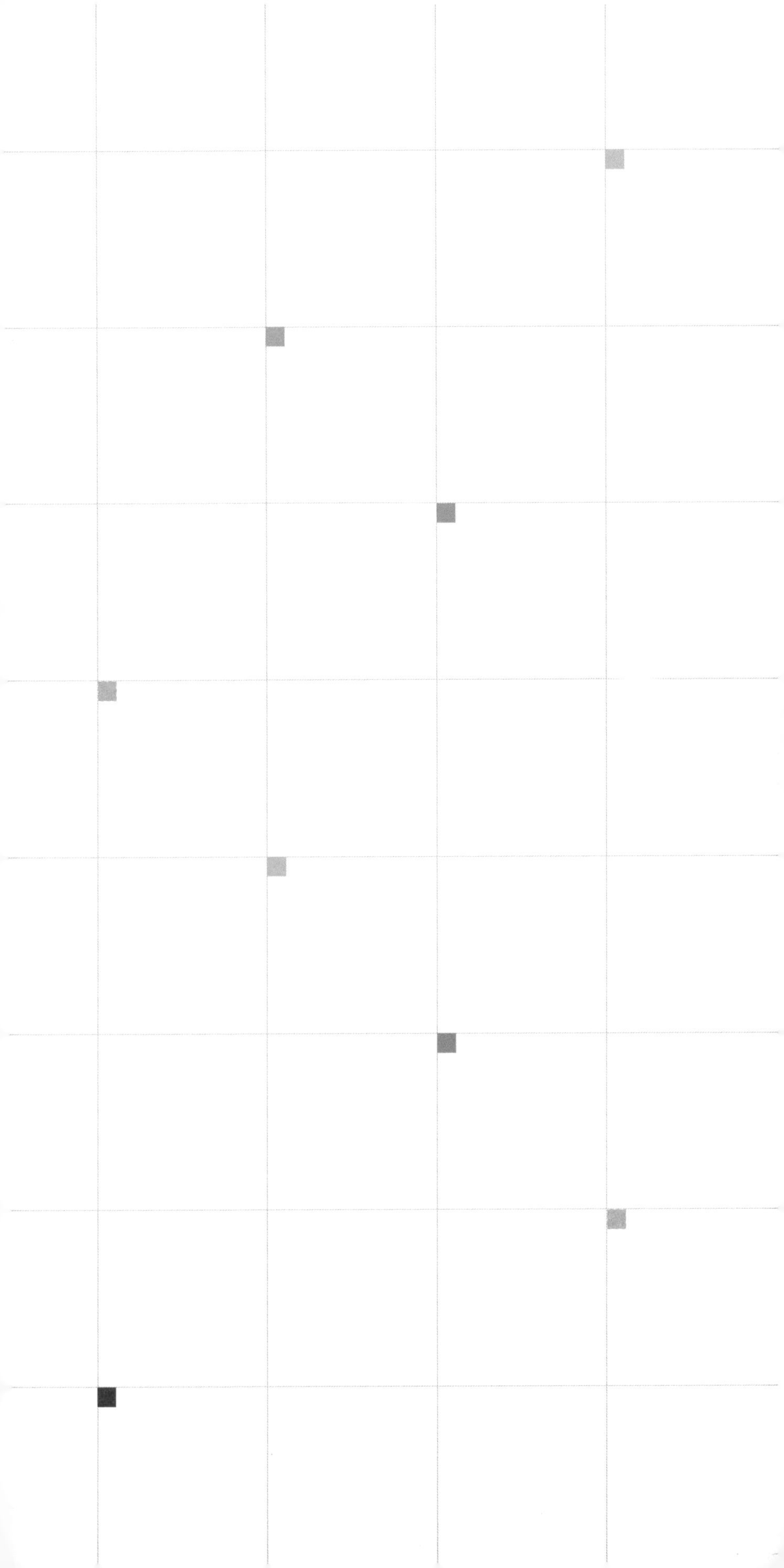

Editor: LAURA DOZIER
Designer: SARAH GIFFORD
Production Manager: ERIN VANDEVEER

Library of Congress Cataloging-in-Publication Data ■

Cooper, Becky.
Mapping Manhattan : a love (and sometimes hate) story in maps by 75 new yorkers /
Becky Cooper.
p. cm.
ISBN 978-1-4197-0672-1
1. Manhattan (New York, N.Y.)—Social life and customs—Anecdotes.
2. New York (N.Y.)—Social life and customs--Anecdotes. 3. New York
(N.Y.)—Biography—Anecdotes. 4. Manhattan (New York, N.Y.)—Maps.
5. New York (N.Y.)—Maps. I. Title.
F128.36.C66 2013
974.7'1—dc23
201203316

Illustrations by Bonnie Briant

Portions of this book originally appeared in different form in the spring 2010 issue of *The Harvard Advocate*.

Printed and bound in China ■ 10 9 8 7 6 5 4 3 2

ABRAMS
THE ART OF BOOKS SINCE 1949
115 West 18th Street
New York, NY 10011
www.abramsbooks.com

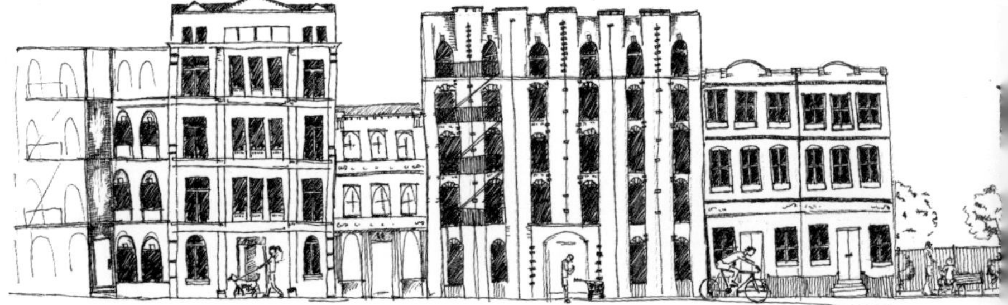

Mapping Manhattan

A Love (and Sometimes Hate) Story in Maps by 75 New Yorkers

Becky Cooper

FOREWORD BY ADAM GOPNIK

ABRAMS IMAGE, NEW YORK

Foreword BY ADAM GOPNIK

Maps and memories are bound together, a little as songs and love affairs are. The artifact envelops the emotion, and then the emotion stores away in the artifact: We hear "All the Things You Are" or "Hey There Delilah" just by chance while we're in love, and then the love is forever after stored in the song. (Someone mentioned this once to Marcel Proust, and he said there might be an idea for a book in it.) So with maps: We go to live somewhere, and then we see a schematic representation of it, and superimposing our memories upon it, we find that it becomes peculiarly . . . *alive*. ■ This attachment requires no particular creative energy. It just happens. Even a map of the most ordinary "found" kind—that map of Schenectady you needed when you went on a bus trip—becomes filled with a particular time's particular pleasure. And (this is the truly weird thing) the more limited the map, the bigger the feelings it evokes. I can't see the métro map of Paris, or hear the roster of its stops—Château Rouge, Gare de l'Est, Château d'Eau—without feeling myself in Paris on a summer Sunday on the way to the flea market. The map is a stronger version of the trip than a video might be; it is almost a stronger version of the trip than the trip is. What's more, I look at the subway map of New York, see the dull line of New York numbers—33, 42, 51, 59—and they fill up at once with memory. Maps, especially schematic ones, are the places where memories go *not* to die, or be pinned, but to live forever.

What's true even of the utilitarian map is still more true of the purpose-made poetic map. Of all artists, Saul Steinberg is the greatest and wittiest poet of the relation between the made map and memories. The most famous of his maps, of course, is of the relation between the New Yorker's mind and the map he makes of the world, with Tenth and Eleventh Avenues looming vast in the foreground and then the rest of America a vaguely sketched-in space, half the size of Manhattan. But this is only one of a hundred equally beautiful maps Steinberg made of his New York, all turning on his own home, on East 75th Street, as the city's natural center. His essential conviction was that we can only live within maps—and that every good map is oriented around our own hearth. It's no accident that Steinberg never drew a landscape, except as nostalgic parody or kitsch pastiche, because the landscape is the antithesis of the map. The usual way of writing the history of images is to insist that the map comes first and the landscape is the escape from it: We start with stylized, conceptual depictions of our world—the ocean chart for the Phoenician sailor showing the way home, the quick charcoal sketch of the bisons' location drawn on the side of the cave—and slowly begin to see, and then show, the elements that maps can't capture, the irreducible optical presence of the world as it really is; this leaf, this shadow, this morning, this one animal. But there is another way of thinking about this: The landscape may be the artificial, warped, artistic vision—earned by hard mental work on the part of creator and beholder both—while the map is the real thing, the way we see, the way we store, and the way we keep it safe for good. Unroll the canvases lined up, without their stretchers, from the artistic attic of our minds, and what we find are not pictures but depictions, not snapshots but, if you like, map-shots, graphic studies of the relationships forged in memory that let us go on, and move on. This is not a conceit, or not *merely* one, nor even a metaphor. Cognitive science now insists that our minds make maps before they take snapshots, storing in schematic form the information we need to navigate and make sense of the world. Maps are our first mental language, not our latest. The photographic sketch, with its optical hesitations, is a thing we force from history; the map, with its neat certainties and foggy edges, looks like the way we think.

Between the found descriptive map we share and the poetic map of the artist lie the smaller improvised personal maps that fill this book—the maps we can't help but make in our heads, even if we don't always draw them with our hands. Manhattan is a particularly fit, rich subject for the mental map. Though big in area, it is small, compressed in articulation. More than almost any other city, it was made on purpose. London is a collection of villages drawing ever more tightly together over time—Shoreditch, where Shakespeare lived, and Southwark, where he worked, about two miles away, were once felt to be as far apart as Montauk and Westhampton, which have some forty miles separating them; Paris, despite the broad boulevards that cut across it, is still an organic web of small streets that seem to supply an overcharge of memory in themselves. New York offers instead a rectilinear grid of numbers and minimal descriptors, a cookie cutter laid down upon a green island. Its most emotive locales are laconically named: Say, Central Park West and 72nd Street. Manhattan is so like the abstract, modernist grid on which Cubist painters were expected to hang their emotions, or objects, in fact, that it isn't an accident that great Cubist paintings, though made in gray Parisian garrets, always put us (as they put their painters) in mind of New York: Song lyrics and old guitars and breakfast tabletops appear through the rigid conceptual scheme of straight verticals and horizontals. And no accident, either, that the New York paintings of Cubist-minded Piet Mondrian, after his immigration here in the 1940s, are among the best mental maps we have of the city, with their perfect evocation of the collision of a high modern sensibility, their taste for geometric abstraction, and a just-off-the-boat arrival's excitement at the blinking, boogie-woogie energy of New York. ■ In Seth Robbins and Robert Neuwirth's wonderful anthology, *Mapping New York*, we see how pliable, how supple this strict ironwork grid has been to the needs and urgencies of individual imaginations, some worthy and some seedy. The nineteenth-century "fire insurance" maps of New York—marvelously detailed and purely utilitarian in purpose, they were used by insurance companies to decide how much coverage to write for each building depending on how close it was to fire departments and gas and water sources—still give a dazzling, rococo view of New York: By miniaturizing the city, they make us specially aware of the variety that lingers within the grid. Filled with seemingly indigestible detail, they remind us of what a varied feast a city is. In a way, these most utilitarian maps of New York provide a stronger and more emotional charge than the more self-consciously wrought city maps do.

It is this essential mapmaker's understanding—that the more restricted the compass it circumscribes, the richer the index of emotion it supplies—that moves Becky Cooper, a young artist and writer of extraordinary gifts and gumption, throughout this book. She had the simple idea of seeding, Johnny Appleseed–like, an extremely schematic map of Manhattan throughout the city, urging its finders to mark their memories on its plain outlines. Later, she asked some better-known New Yorkers to join the game. What is startling throughout is how much emotion pours through the limited language of pure mapping. A remembered relation of spaces, a hole, a circle, a shaded area—and a whole life comes alive. The real appeal of the map, perhaps, is not so much that it stores our past as that it forces our emotions to be pressed into their most parsimonious essence—and, as every poet knows, it is emotion under the force of limits, emotion pressed down and held down to strict formal constraints, that makes for the purest expression. These maps are street haiku, whose emotions, whether made by the well known or the anonymous, are more moving for being so stylized. My life? You can reduce it to this series of marks right here—and once reduced, it has more of its essential tang and meaning, not less. ■ In their abstract, conceptual simplicity, the maps remind us of what a consensual thing a city is, particularly one as plural as New York. We make it up together. We scrutinize that map on the subway wall before we find our own apartment, and then start to make up newer maps where that apartment becomes, for our New York, the San Marco of everything, the central piazza.

"I see buildings and water" were the haunting, inescapable last words of the flight attendant on 9/11 who did not know where she was. Cities, when we see them, seem first like chaos and have to be revealed to us as charts before we know them as our own. The spare, topographic facts speak, and love (and some torch) songs then pour out. In the face of mortality, we turn those buildings, that water, first into a map, and then a memory, and at last, a life. Each map in this book diagrams the one thing we most want a map to show us, and that is a way home.

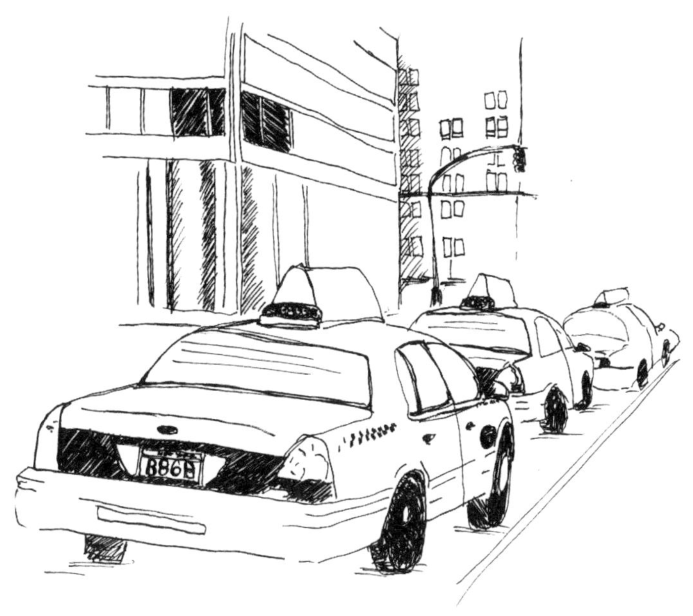

Making Invisible Cities Visible

All maps tell stories. Stories of their mapmakers. Stories about the circumstances of their creation. Stories about their intended use. They're all biased in some way. Even the subway map of New York—the iconic John Tauranac blue-beige one that hangs in every subway car—is distorted. Manhattan is squished. Downtown luxuriates while poor Inwood and Washington Heights, served only by the 1 and A trains, are forced to fit into a fraction of the space they would actually take. And yet, for many, this map *is* New York City.

Five years ago, I accidentally became a cartographer. The summer after my freshman year of college, I was hired to design a 90-inch-long map of all the public art in Manhattan. My job was, technically, to write the copy that accompanied the map, but on the first day, my boss took me over to her computer. She opened the map in Illustrator and the program self-destructed. The file was too large. ■ I spent the whole summer fixing that map. I placed 1,500 dots for the city's public sculptures, subway mosaics, and murals. I color-coded every dot, placed a thumbnail image for each, and cross-referenced them all according to provenance. I dreamed about those dots. ■ By the end, the map was a beast. There was so much information on it that it was hardly legible. But at least it was done. ■ As I was cleaning my desk that final day, I came across napkins I'd drawn on over the course of the summer. They were filled with tiny maps of the city. I'd sketched them to help me get from work to dinner or a park concert or a friend's house; I'm terrible at geography, and this was before I had a smartphone. As I looked through the pile, I realized the maps were a record of my summer. Beyond that, they provided a more honest picture of Manhattan than the giant one I'd been slaving over. For all its unwieldiness and all my attempts at objectivity, the giant map was still a reflection of me—I was making subjective decisions about what "public" meant (for example, the paintings in city schools: should they be considered public?) and about what counted as art (a carousel?). Instead of making the map thorough and unbiased, the amount of information I crammed on the page muddled the portrait of the city. ■ I decided that in order to make a map that told an honest story of a place, I would need to celebrate—not hide—the subjectivity of the mapmaker. Instead of striving for one giant, "complete" map, I should aim for many little portraits. I would ask people to map the essence of who they are and what a location is to them, and out of the mosaic of these personal visions, the place would emerge. ■ It would be a literal version of Italo Calvino's *Invisible Cities*, a series of portraits of fantastic and fantastical cities as told by Marco Polo to Kublai Khan. Polo vividly recounts tales of the cities he encountered on his explorations—one that smells of elephants after the rain, one where desire is already a memory. Near the end, Kublai Khan asks why the explorer's tales describe cities in every corner of his empire but never Venice. Polo smiles and says, "What else do you believe I have been talking to you about?" All these cities are, in fact, portraits of Venice from different points of view. ■ "So yours is truly a journey through memory!" Kublai Khan exclaims. ■ Map Your Memories, the collaborative public art project from which this book emerged, was born.

NEW YORK

My family immigrated to the Lower East Side of Manhattan: my father's grandparents from Russia in the 1890s, my mother's parents from China in the 1920s and '40s. After moving from the other side of the world, they were tired of schlepping, and stayed. I like to imagine the two sides bumping into each other, unknowingly, in front of Hop Kee on Mott Street, which my mother's father would pass after closing his watch repair shop on the corner of Mott and Worth and where my dad's father used to eat after his Broadway show let out. ■ Since then, New York has seeped into my family's blood. For her eighty-fifth birthday, my grandmother asked me to take her around to jazz clubs in the West Village. She still jaywalks at busy intersections and taps honking cabs with her cane: "Hey, dontcha see me crossing here?" ■ Where else but New York, then, would I start the project? It's a city so iconic, so full of romance and mystery, that it means something different to everyone. I wanted to make our invisible cities, our private New Yorks—the ones lurking behind the places we live, the ones secretly populating the street corners and stores we pass every day—visible. ■ But Queens, my home; the Bronx; Staten Island; and dear, dear Brooklyn would have to wait. I wanted to start where the city began: Manhattan.

THE MAPS

The island I printed looks, as Truman Capote once put it, like "a diamond iceberg" floating between the East and Hudson Rivers. Or as Pat Flanagan wrote in his postcard to me, months after I handed him a map, like "an abdomen without the appendages necessary for life" or "a leg of lamb" one meat hook shy of a slaughterhouse (see page 59). I think it looks more like a jalapeño pepper, with a vein down the middle for Broadway, a horizontal slice of a knife for Houston Street, and a rectangular blemish for Central Park. These three marks are the essence of Manhattan's geography: Broadway, the avenue that runs the length of the island and ignores the grid; Houston, where the grid starts; and Central Park, the great exception to the urban pattern. There's also a baby pepper, or maybe a stray leaf, by Manhattan's side: Roosevelt Island. ■ I printed each map by hand on the letterpress in the basement of my college dorm. (The movable lead type was down the hall from the vending machines. We also had an old Puzzle Bobble arcade machine, a swimming pool converted into a theater, and giant painted tunnels whose walls read, "Kisses are a better fate than wisdom." It was a weird, wonderful place.) I wanted the map to have a physicality, to be an object, to slow the recipients down and make them truly think about their relationships with this city. I passed each sheet of paper through three times: once for the address, once for the debossed quadrille pattern that would play with the city's grid, and once for the base map. ■ The maps were like passports into strangers' worlds. I distributed them by walking down Broadway and across Houston and by winding through Central Park. I gave them to as wide a variety of New Yorkers as I could find: a psychic on St. Mark's, a dreadlocks barber in the East Village, a curator at the Museum of Art and Design whom I caught as she was about to twist into the revolving door of the museum. Sometimes I chose a person because her heels were awesome. Or because he was carrying a plastic tube, and I was hoping he was an architect. But most of the time, I just chose people who looked open to the world—without headphones, curious. ■ I talked to gas station workers, MTA employees, artists, tourists, and veterans; to Columbia med students, Mister Softee drivers, city planners, San Francisco quilters, bakery owners, street cart vendors, Central Park portraitists, jazz musicians, *Watchtower* distributors, undergrads, can collectors, and mail carriers. Watching their cynicism melt, hearing them—against all odds—thank me for the chance to map their city, I forgot about all the hours I had spent in the basement, printing by letterpress, and the calluses I still had on my hands.

THE BOOK

These are their maps. Their ghosts. Their past loves. Their secret spots. Their favorite restaurants. These are their accidental autobiographies; when people don't realize they're revealing themselves, they're apt to lay themselves much more bare. These are vignettes of their lives. A study of the kinds of memories that stick over the years. This is Manhattan from those who know it best. ■ Tucked among the anonymous maps are those of notable New Yorkers. Yoko Ono shares her memory lane, and Harvey Fierstein maps his trysts. Philippe Petit tightrope-walks, once again, between the Twin Towers, and the *New Yorker*'s Patricia Marx loses her mind and her virginity. There are also the maps of the New Yorkers behind New York: The head of the Public Library's map division. The director of the American Museum of Natural History's planetarium. A former police lieutenant who responded to the call on 9/11. I've aimed for celebrities and for Manhattan's characters, for people in the map world and for people integral to New York history. ■ The narrative moves from Manhattan at 228th Street to Battery Park, because to travel south on Broadway is to travel back in time. It is told as a single day, though in reality, I handed out maps on multiple full-day marathons down Broadway and across the island. I've tried to be as accurate as possible with the locations and the dialogue of the people I met. But forgive me if I moved you from Central Park to Broadway for dramatic simplicity. ■ The maps are organized roughly geographically (the Plaza map, page 74, is as near as I could get it to 59th Street), mostly thematically (how could I resist pairing the simplicity of "Met My Wife," page 66, with the cheekiness of "Wives & Lovers," page 67), and always visually. I've tried to zoom in from the overview to the intimate, and back out from the personal to the collective. The maps are interspersed with sketches of everyday New York scenes and anecdotes from the characters I encountered. I want you to experience handing the maps out with me. To meet the people and smell the city. To watch New York slide back in time, noticing how each building has layers of history. I hope to show Manhattan as a cabinet of curiosities, a container of portals to hundreds of worlds; if I've succeeded, this portrait of the city will be as true as any of the seventy-five others. ■ Finally, in the back of the book, there is a blank map for you to fill out and send back, should you be inspired to participate in the project.

MAPPING MANHATTAN

This book, an anthropological fingerprint of the city, is in the tradition of other works of creative cartography, personal mapping, and psychogeography. Stanley Milgram, the social psychologist who realized people were shockingly willing to zap other people with high voltage in lab situations, did a similar project thirty-five years ago in *New York* magazine. It is also a response to the ubiquity and ease of Google Maps—a GPS can't map the cure to all kinds of lostness—and a refusal of the idea that all print can go digital. (Look, I still use the post office!) ■ Beyond this, it's a love letter to New York and to the people who shape it. To a place of restlessness, constant motion, and passion. A city of contradictions. But also to a place that's so much more. ■ I've been thinking a lot about what defines a city. How you can capture its essence. In Portland, people twirl in the streets. In Paris, everything is a gorgeous art museum: Look, don't get too comfortable, and certainly don't change things unnecessarily. But what about Manhattan? Are we New Yorkers characterized by our energy? Our feverishness? Do we all come here seeking something? Do we all have the same fears? The same size dreams? ■ It's taken me twenty years to realize I love this place not just because I was born here. I take pictures of the reservoir in Central Park at sunset, even though I've run there a hundred times before. My heart fills when I hear an older man at City Diner say, "Hey, Marion, have you tried the pies here yet? They're nice." I love the subway. The fleeting moments of connection—a glance with a stranger to acknowledge a rat on the tracks, the hand that goes out of its way to keep the door open for you. Even the gentle white noise of a train rumbling between stations is something I get as homesick for as for my mother's cooking. Maybe that one's just me. ■ And yet, there will always be something essentially *elsewhere* about New York. It is a place that people come to precisely because it doesn't ever fully offer itself. It's intoxicating. Keeps you on your toes. Keeps you drinking coffee and keeps you walking. ■ Part of why I love New York so deeply is exactly this elusiveness. This refusal to be caught is what allows it to carry such fantasy, mystery, and myth, yet also be home. It is simultaneously no one's city and everyone's city. ■ New York may always be just over there, but what you know is *yours*. And these tiny, invisible cities are what make up Manhattan.

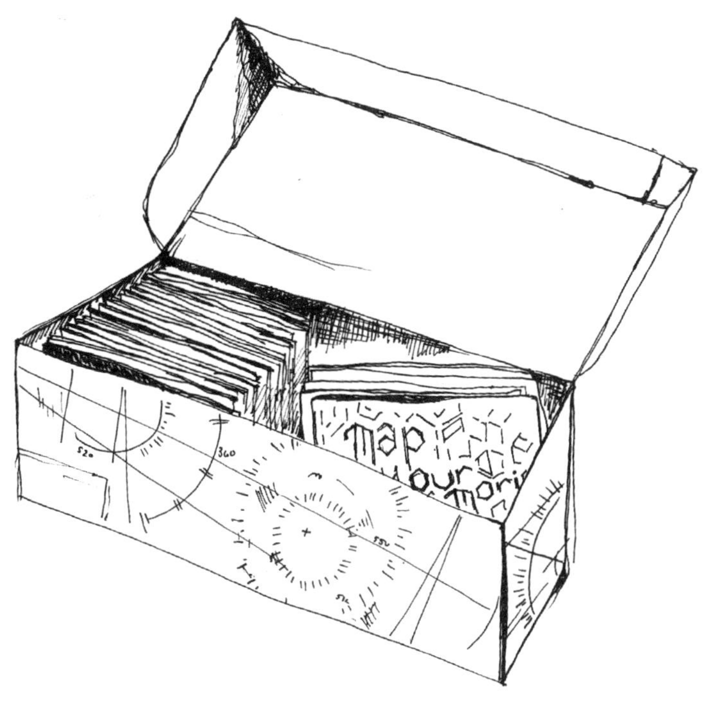

Maps are more about their makers

than the places they describe. ■

Map who you are. ■ *Map where you are.* ■

Fill the whole map with a story

or paint your favorite cup of coffee. ■

Map the invisible. ■ *Map the obvious.*

■ *Map your memories.*

225TH STREET—BROADWAY BRIDGE, 10:25 A.M.
It's a brisk April morning of what is sure to turn into a gorgeous day in New York City, and my roommate, Ama Francis, and I have just gotten off the number 1 train at 231st Street in the Bronx. Sneakers are strapped to our feet, and a shoebox full of blank maps of Manhattan is tucked under my arm. We exit the stairs and turn right to face south on Broadway. Broadway is also US Route 9, and it shows here. The road is a busy two-lane highway, with cars honking and buses speeding by. Pigeons fly toward our heads, and the streets smell like car exhaust despite the pear blossoms and magnolias that line the streets, as they do in much of New York this time of year. ■ We're about to begin our 13.6-mile marathon walk down the length of Broadway, following its transformation from highway to city boulevard, watching it connect commercial glitz to fading history, and trying to piece together the overlooked details that make this island what it is. We're asking strangers to take the maps and send them back, filled with their dreams, memories, secrets . . . anything that makes this place special to them. ■ Just south of 230th Street, we cross an invisible border, the paved-over bend of Spuyten Duyvil Creek, and pass from the Bronx to Manhattan's Marble Hill, a sneaky little part of Manhattan that's not actually connected to the rest of the borough. It dots the *i* of the island. ■ As we approach 225th Street, the looming steel skeleton of the Broadway Bridge forces the sun to play hide-and-seek. The island of Manhattan begins on the other side.

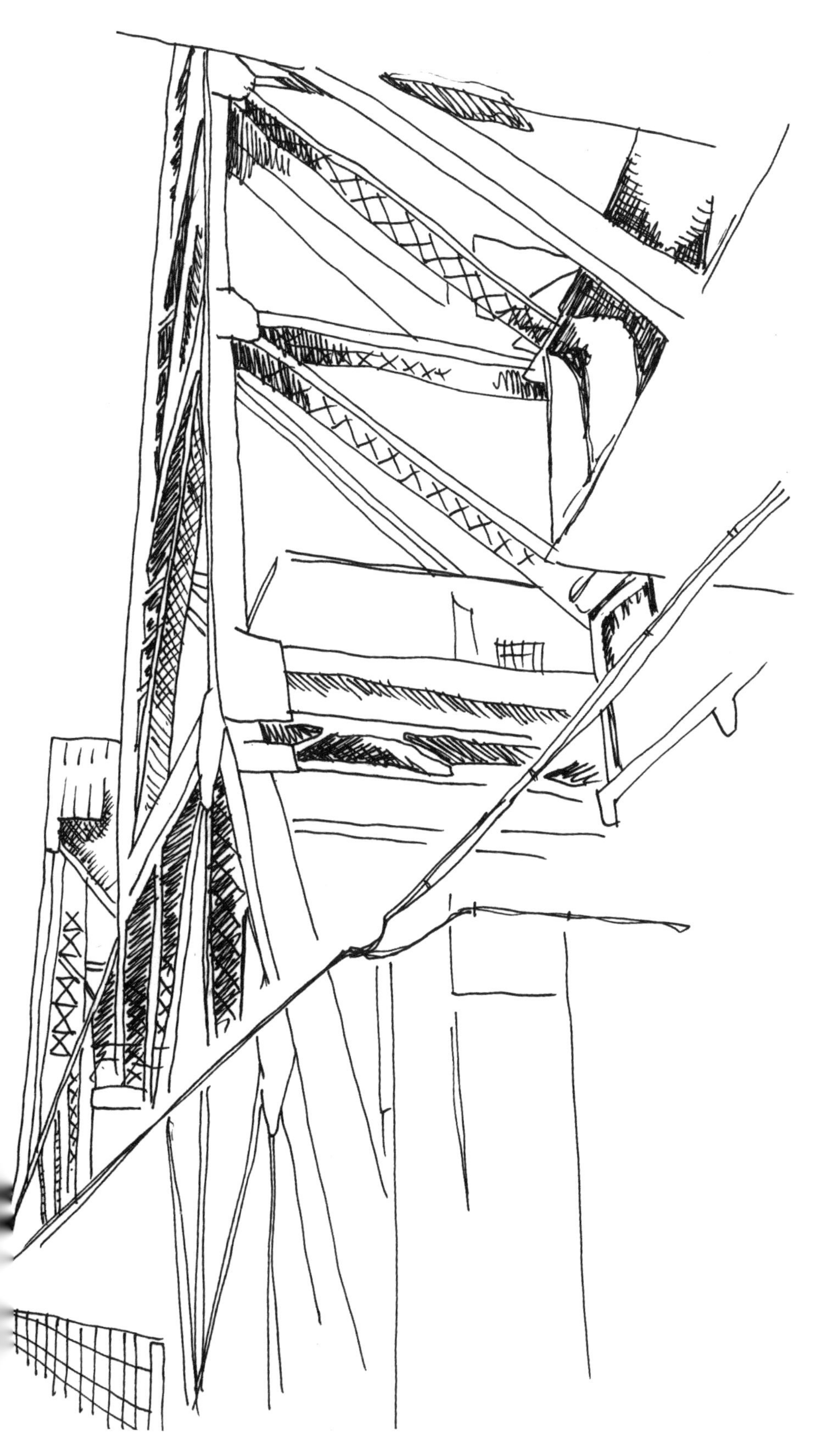

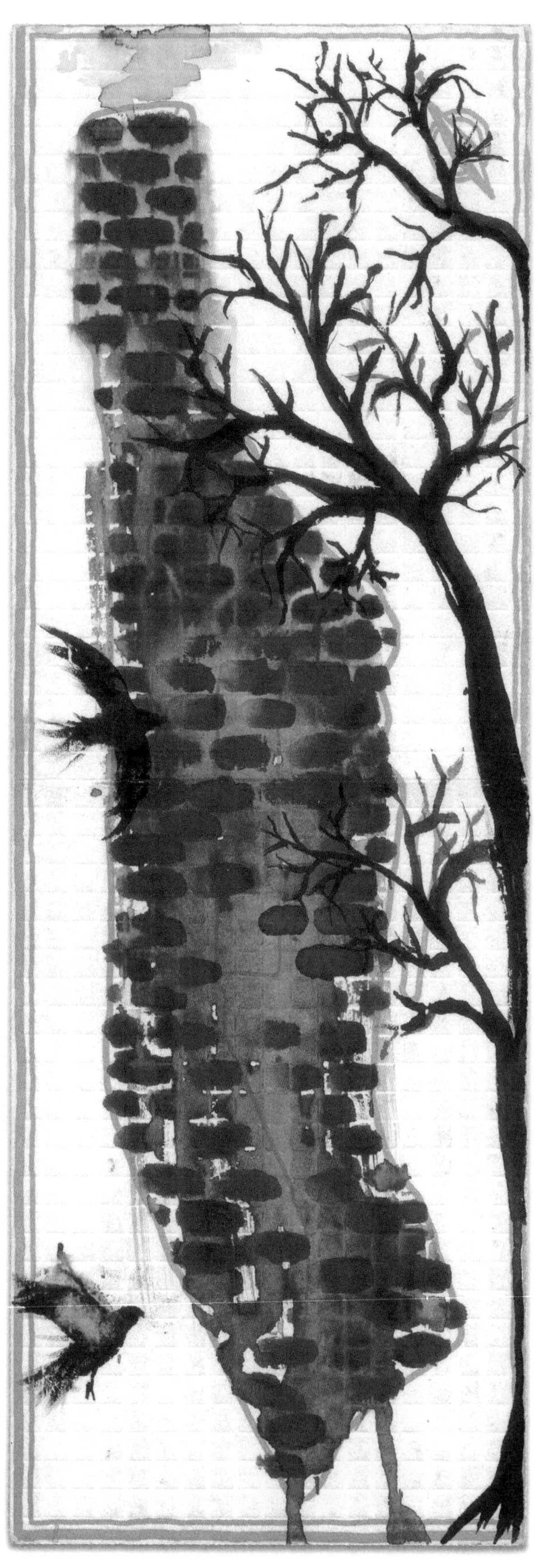

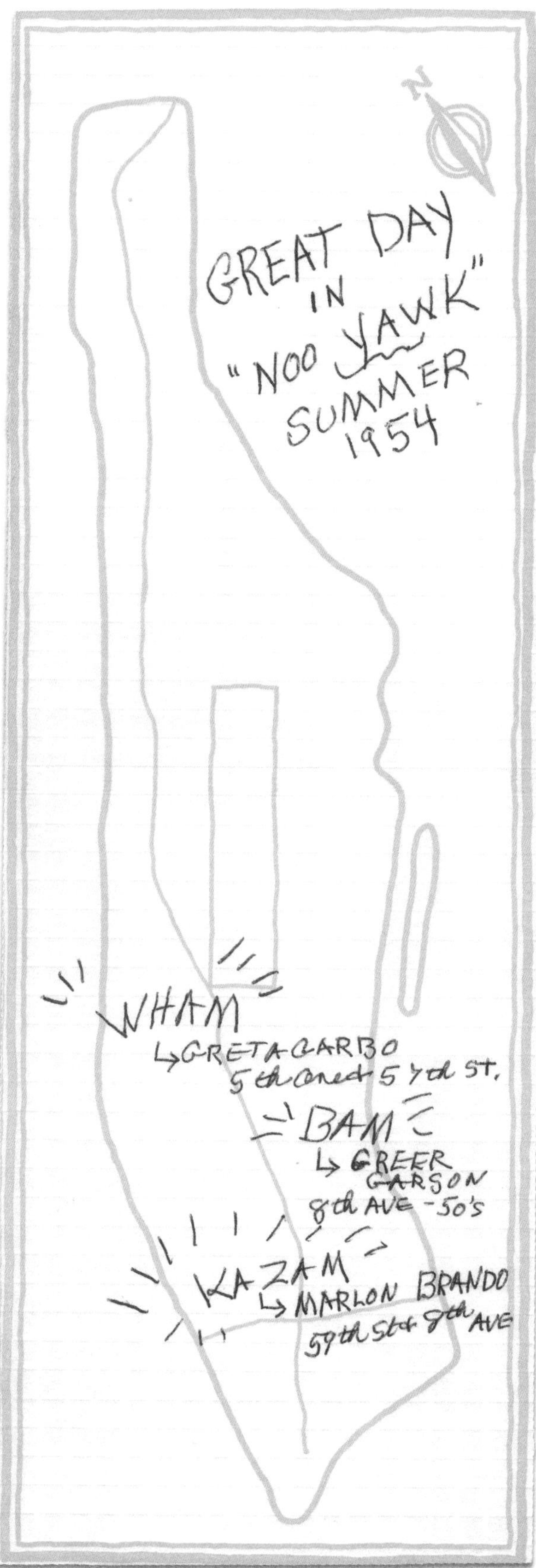
N
GREAT DAY
IN
"NOO YAWK"
SUMMER
1954
WHAM
↳ GRETA GARBO
5th and 57th St.
BAM
↳ GREER
GARSON
8th AVE - 50's
KAZAM
↳ MARLON BRANDO
59th St + 8th AVE

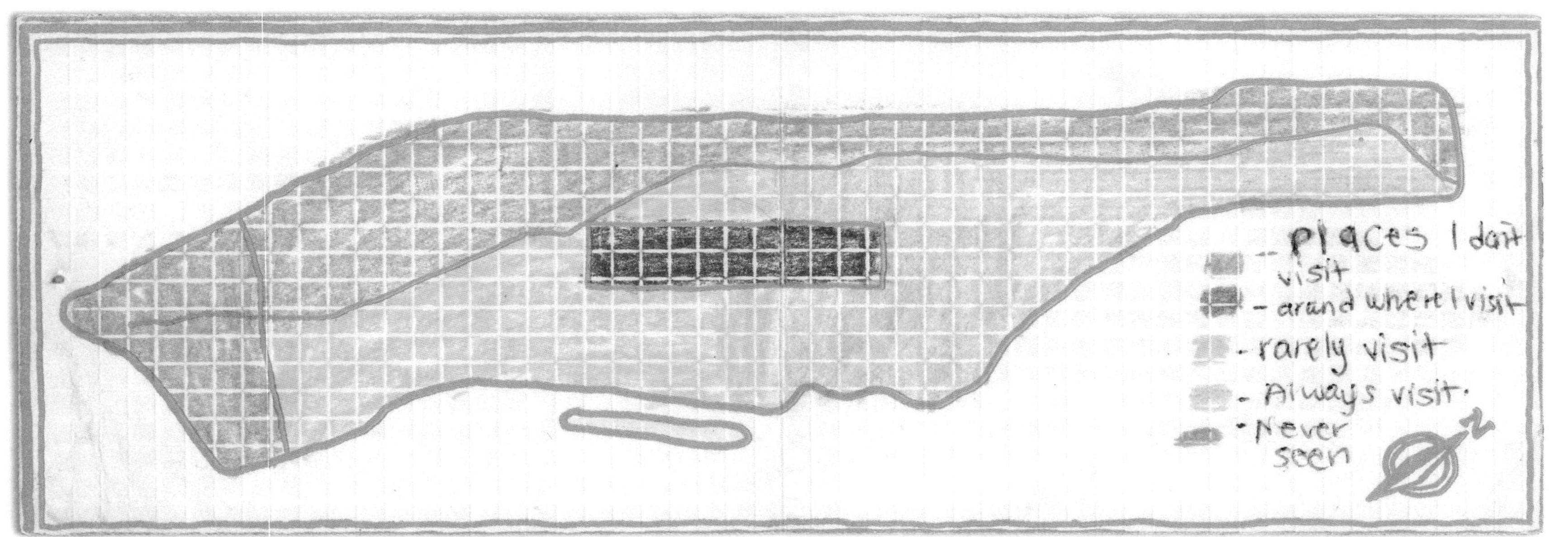
Places I dont visit
- arand where I visit
- rarely visit
- Always visit.
- Never seen
N

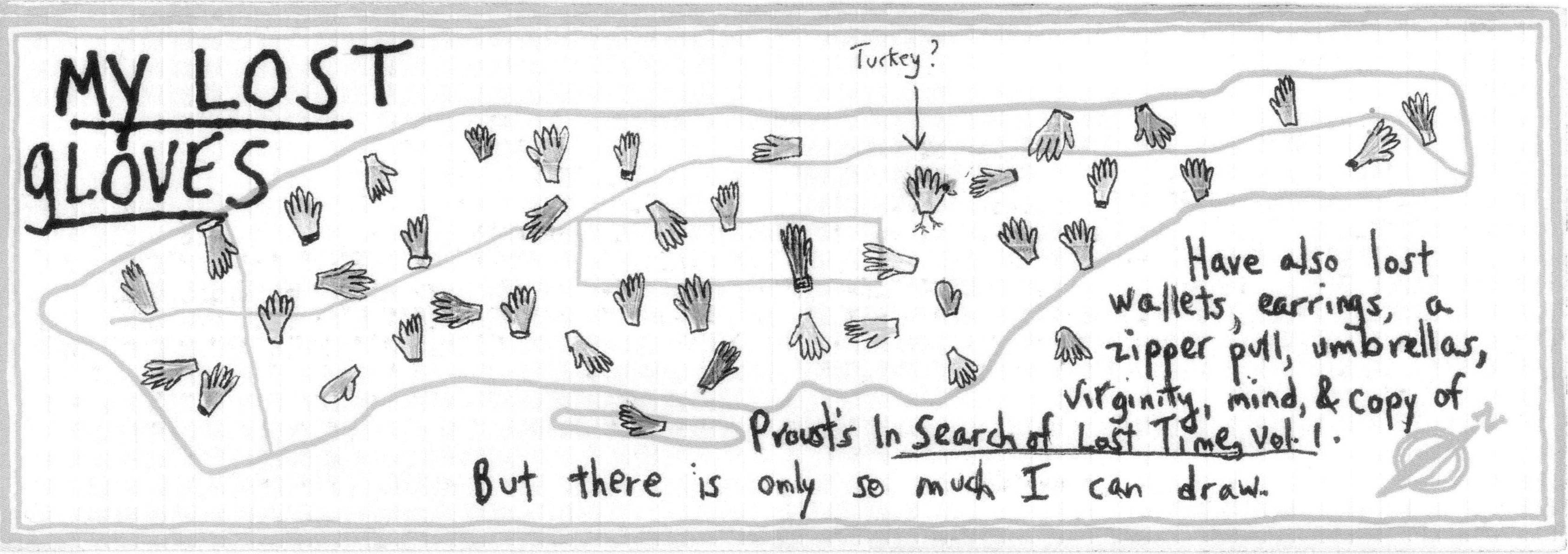
MY LOST GLOVES
Turkey?
Have also lost wallets, earrings, a zipper pull, umbrellas, virginity, mind, & copy of Proust's In Search of Lost Time, Vol. 1.
But there is only so much I can draw.
N

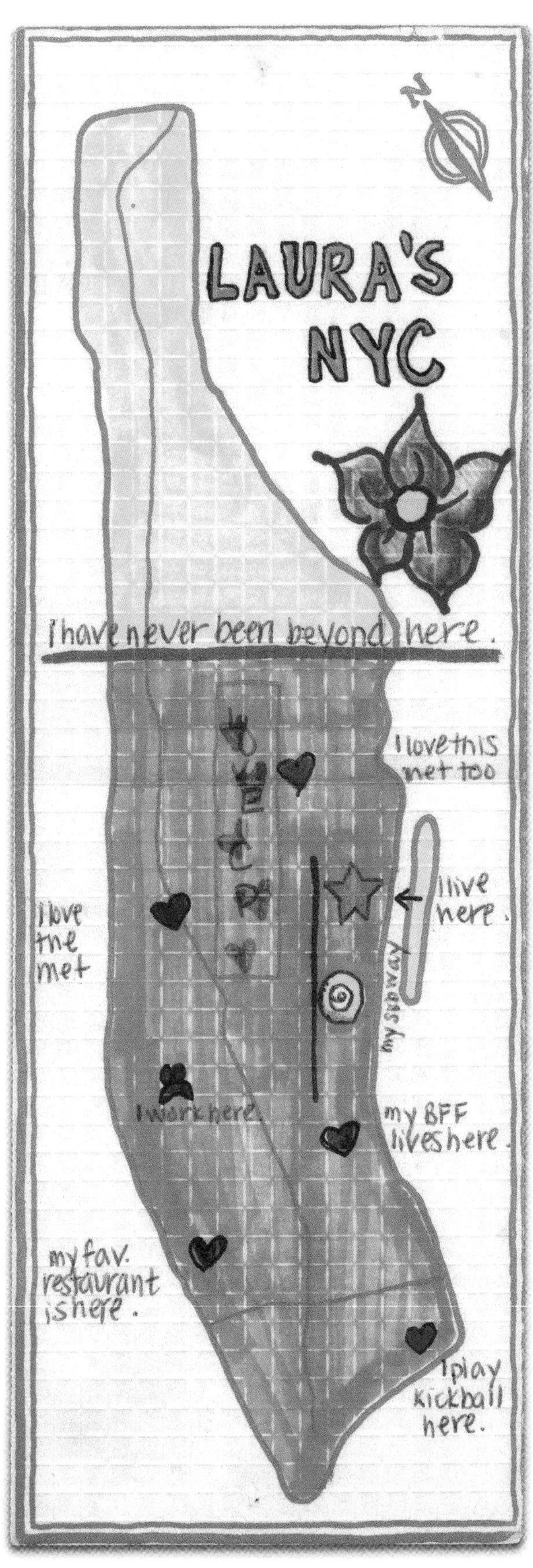
N
LAURA'S
NYC
I have never been beyond here.
I love this met too
I live here.
my subway
I love the met
I work here.
my BFF lives here.
my fav. restaurant is here.
I play kickball here.

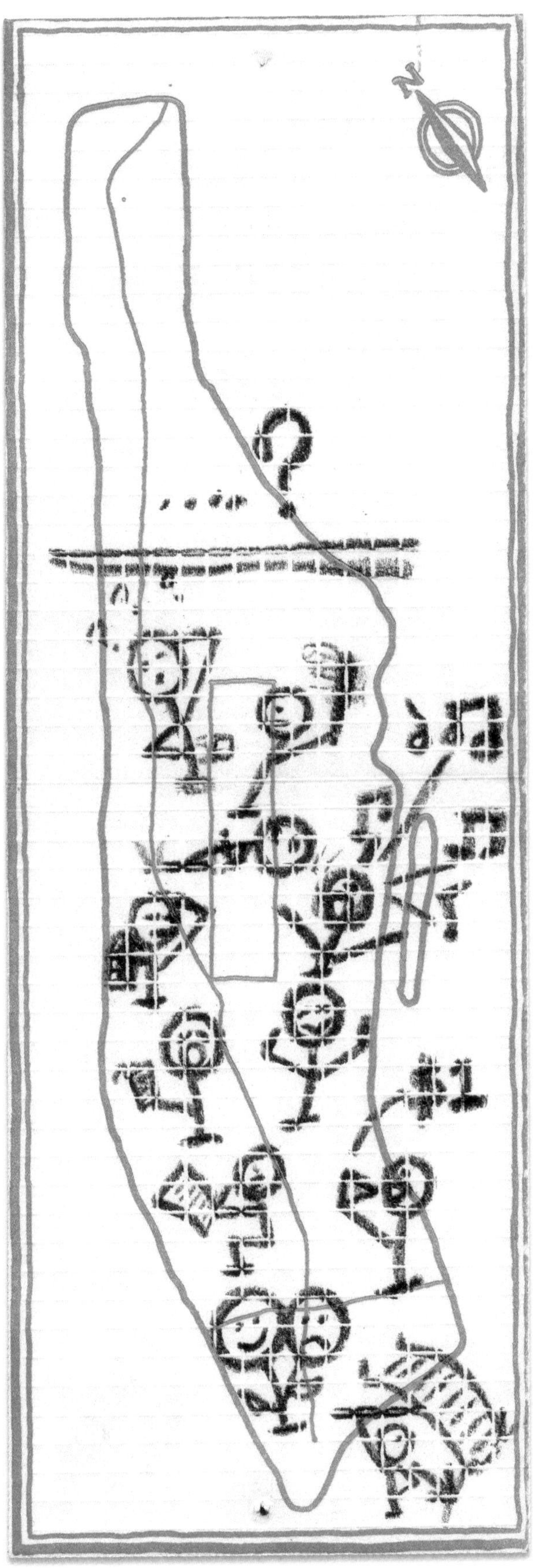
N
#1

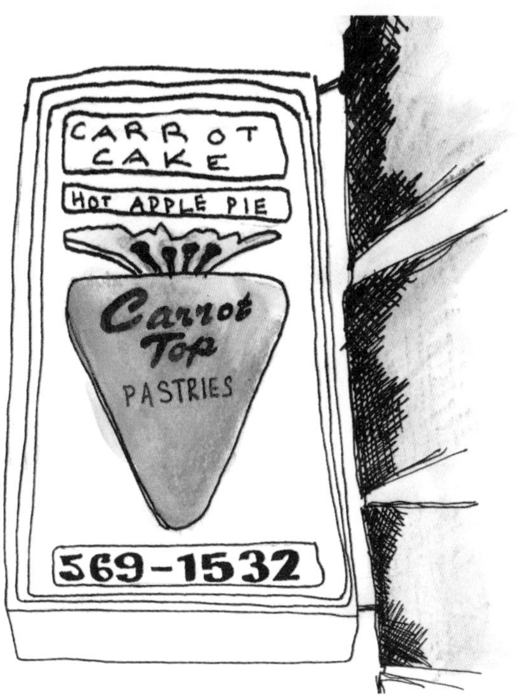

5025 BROADWAY, BETWEEN 214TH AND 215TH STREETS—CARROT TOP PASTRIES, 10:45 A.M.

"No no no. So let me tell you. I did this quiz in the *New York Post*: 'How Much of a New Yorker Are You?' Or some shit. Man, I've lived here my whole life, so I was like, 'I got this shit.' But *shit*, man. The quiz was hard. It's like, *I don't know this stuff*: 'What's the highest subway station in New York?'" ■ I shrug. ■ "Smith-Ninth Street in Brooklyn. *What!*" the man continues, his flailing arms almost thwacking a passerby in a fuchsia jumpsuit. The man doesn't notice. "Who knows that shit? That's not New York. Here's the one I got: What's the only borough that's totally connected to the mainland?" ■ "The Bronx?" I say. ■ "Yeah! My friend lives there 'cause it's the only part of New York that's totally connected to the mainland, so if shit goes down, he can just keep running. You know. 'Cause elsewhere, it'd be like, '*Run—water! Ah!*'" ■ The stranger pretends the boundary of his concrete block is the edge of the island. "*Run!*" He hits the crack in the pavement closest to me. "*Water! Blah!*" He spins 90 degrees and runs north on Broadway—"*Run!*"—until he hits the edge of the concrete tile, spins again over his right shoulder, runs away from me, his black high-tops practically screeching on the pavement—"*Water!*"—spins again, runs. ■ "But in the Bronx he could just keep running." He breathes hard. "9/11 did different things to people." ■ The air hangs above the asphalt, thick enough to stir. ■ "Anyway, girl, I'll take your map. I'll do it for you. You want me to map the shit that means something to me? What Manhattan is for me? Okay. You got it, babe. Good luck."

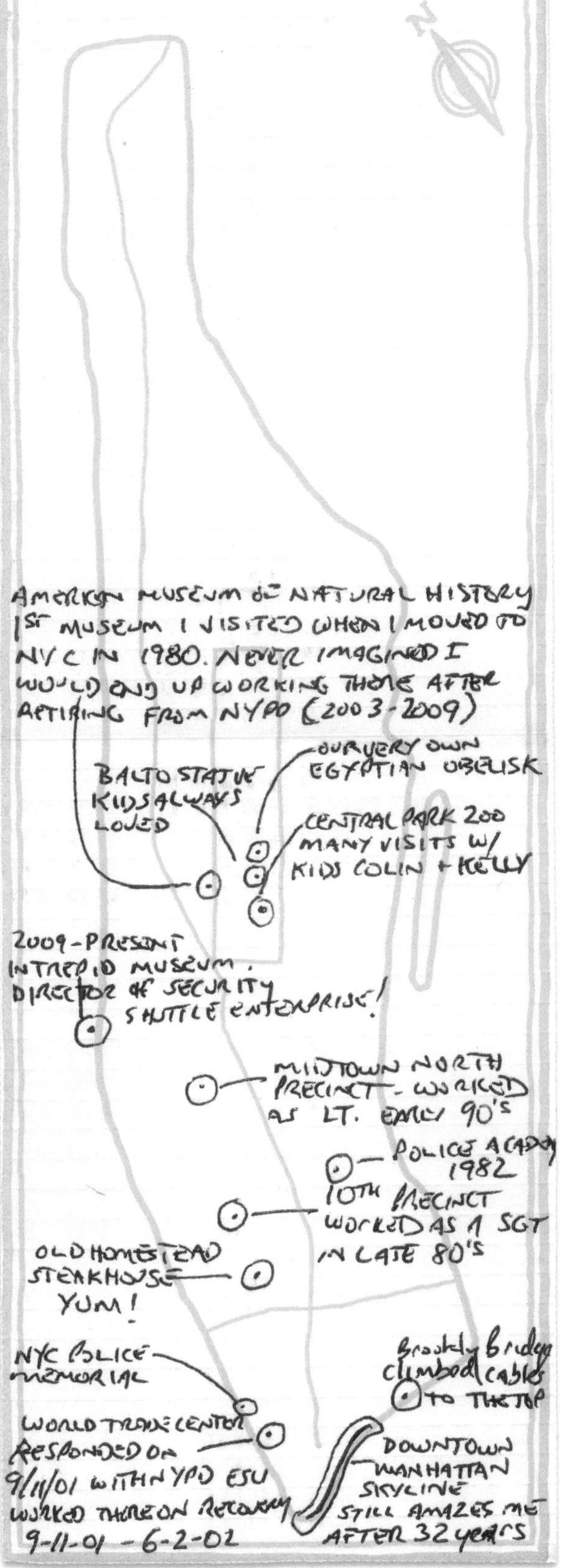
N
AMERICAN MUSEUM OF NATURAL HISTORY
1ST MUSEUM I VISITED WHEN I MOVED TO
NYC IN 1980. NEVER IMAGINED I
WOULD END UP WORKING THERE AFTER
RETIRING FROM NYPD (2003-2009)
OUR VERY OWN
EGYPTIAN OBELISK
BALTO STATUE
KIDS ALWAYS
LOVED
CENTRAL PARK ZOO
MANY VISITS W/
KIDS COLIN + KELLY
2009-PRESENT
INTREPID MUSEUM.
DIRECTOR OF SECURITY
SHUTTLE ENTERPRISE!
MIDTOWN NORTH
PRECINCT - WORKED
AS LT. EARLY 90'S
POLICE ACADEMY
1982
10TH PRECINCT
WORKED AS A SGT
IN LATE 80'S
OLD HOMESTEAD
STEAKHOUSE
YUM!
NYC POLICE
MEMORIAL
Brooklyn Bridge
climbed cables
TO THE TOP
WORLD TRADE CENTER
RESPONDED ON
9/11/01 WITH NYPD ESU
WORKED THERE ON RECOVERY
9-11-01 - 6-2-02
DOWNTOWN
MANHATTAN
SKYLINE
STILL AMAZES ME
AFTER 32 years

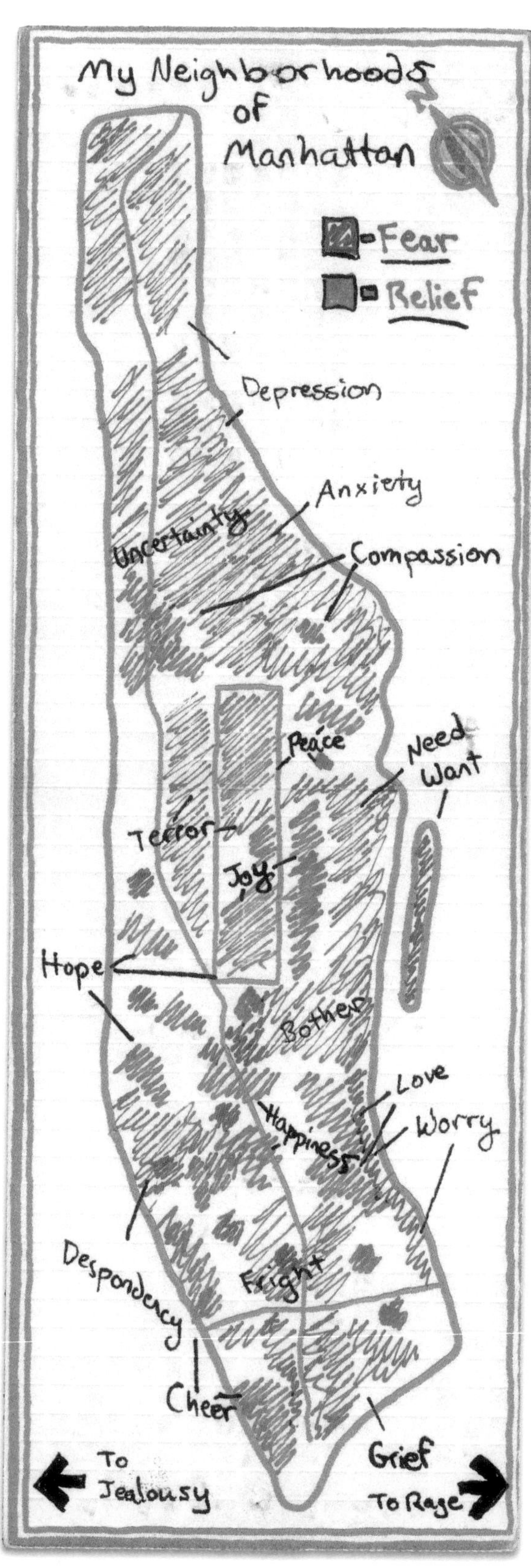
My Neighborhoods
of
Manhattan
Fear
Relief
Depression
Anxiety
Uncertainty
Compassion
Peace
Need
Want
Terror
Joy
Hope
Bother
Love
Happiness
Worry
Despondency
Fright
Cheer
Grief
To
Jealousy
To Rage

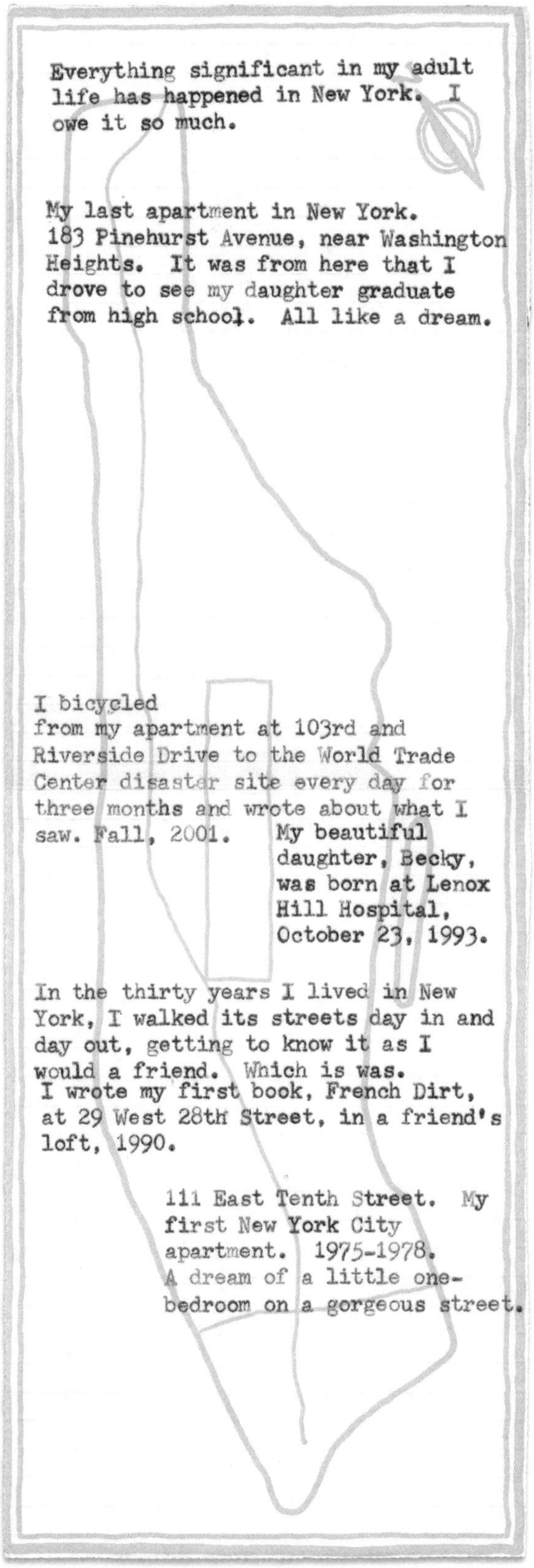

Everything significant in my adult life has happened in New York. I owe it so much.

My last apartment in New York. 183 Pinehurst Avenue, near Washington Heights. It was from here that I drove to see my daughter graduate from high school. All like a dream.

I bicycled from my apartment at 103rd and Riverside Drive to the World Trade Center disaster site every day for three months and wrote about what I saw. Fall, 2001.

My beautiful daughter, Becky, was born at Lenox Hill Hospital, October 23, 1993.

In the thirty years I lived in New York, I walked its streets day in and day out, getting to know it as I would a friend. Which is was.

I wrote my first book, French Dirt, at 29 West 28th Street, in a friend's loft, 1990.

111 East Tenth Street. My first New York City apartment. 1975-1978. A dream of a little one-bedroom on a gorgeous street.

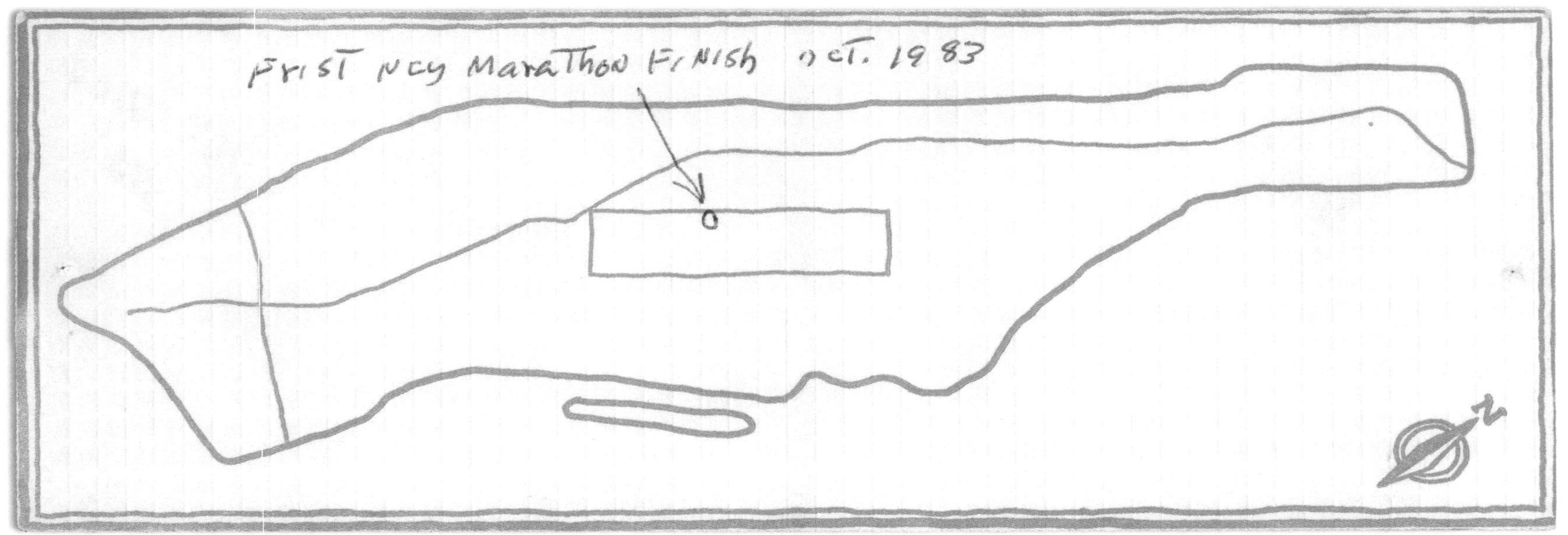
FrisT NCY MaraThon FiNISh OcT. 1983
N

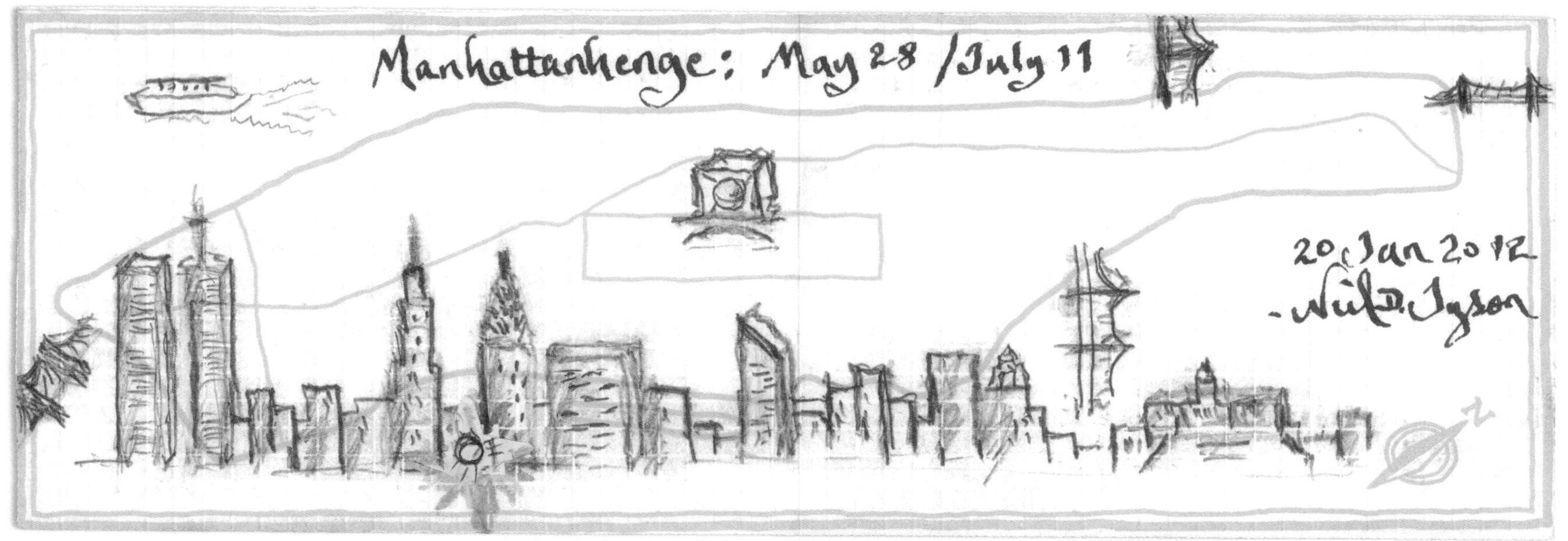

NEIL DEGRASSE TYSON

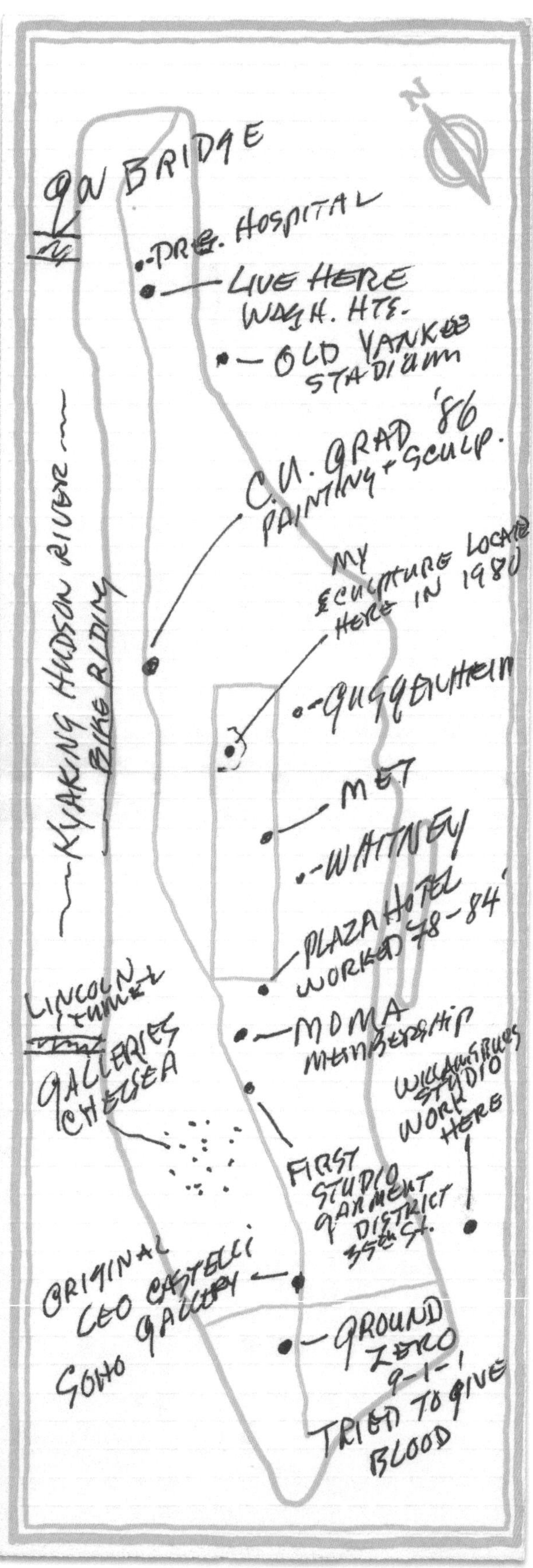
N
GW BRIDGE
PRES. HOSPITAL
LIVE HERE
WASH. HTS.
OLD YANKEE
STADIUM
C.U. GRAD '86
PAINTING + SCULP.
MY
SCULPTURE LOCATED
HERE IN 1980
KYAKING HUDSON RIVER
BIKE RIDING
GUGGENHEIM
MET
WHITNEY
PLAZA HOTEL
WORKED 78-84'
LINCOLN
TUNNEL
MOMA
MEMBERSHIP
GALLERIES
CHELSEA
WILLIAMSBURG
STUDIO
WORK
HERE
FIRST
STUDIO
GARMENT
DISTRICT
35th ST.
ORIGINAL
LEO CASTELLI
GALLERY
SOHO
GROUND
ZERO
9-1-1
TRIED TO GIVE
BLOOD

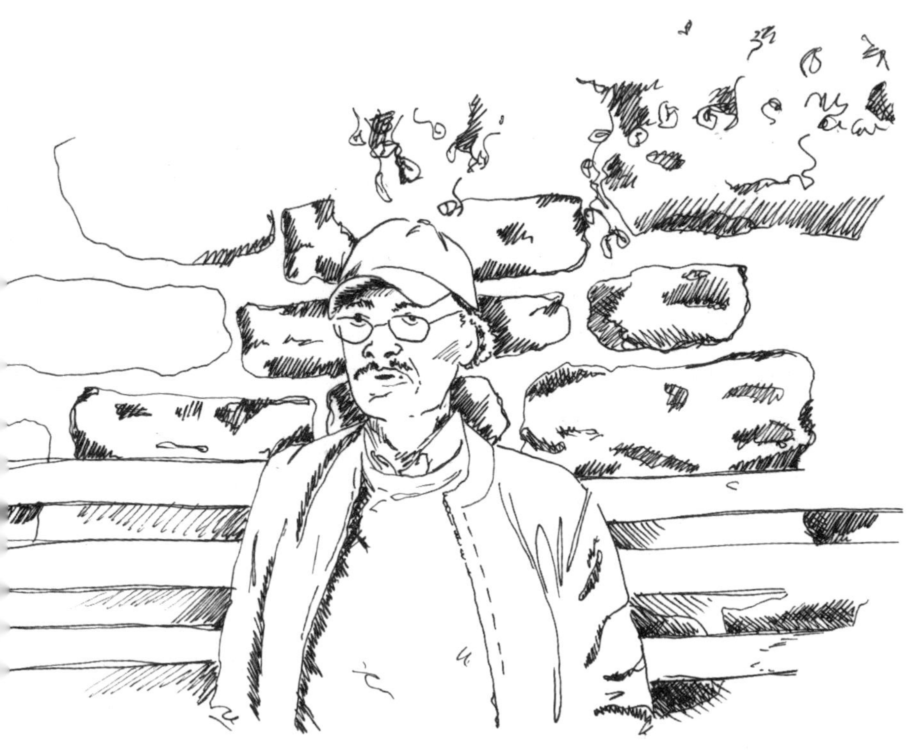

212TH STREET—FOOT OF ISHAM PARK, 10:55 A.M.

We meet Ken just south of 212th Street. He is sitting on a bench in the dappled shade, enjoying the company of an elegant older woman in a ruby coat. ■ "I'm doing an art project where I'm asking people to fill out blank maps of Manhattan . . . ," I explain when I reach their bench. ■ "I know New York," Ken jumps in. "I been living here seventy-two years." He pauses, flashing his gummy smile. "You know New York–Presbyterian Hospital? That's where the Yankees played before they had Yankee Stadium. No one knows that." ■ He's right. The New York Highlanders, as they were then called, played in Hilltop Park, which spanned the area from 165th to 168th Streets. The lot later laid vacant until the hospital claimed the space. ■ "My mother moved there," he says, pointing across the street, "and I was up in the Bronx. But in 1971, when she got sick, I came back to Inwood. I'm living in New York all my life. All my life. My kids were born here. And my son is almost fifty-four. Yeah. I'll fill it out with all I've got."

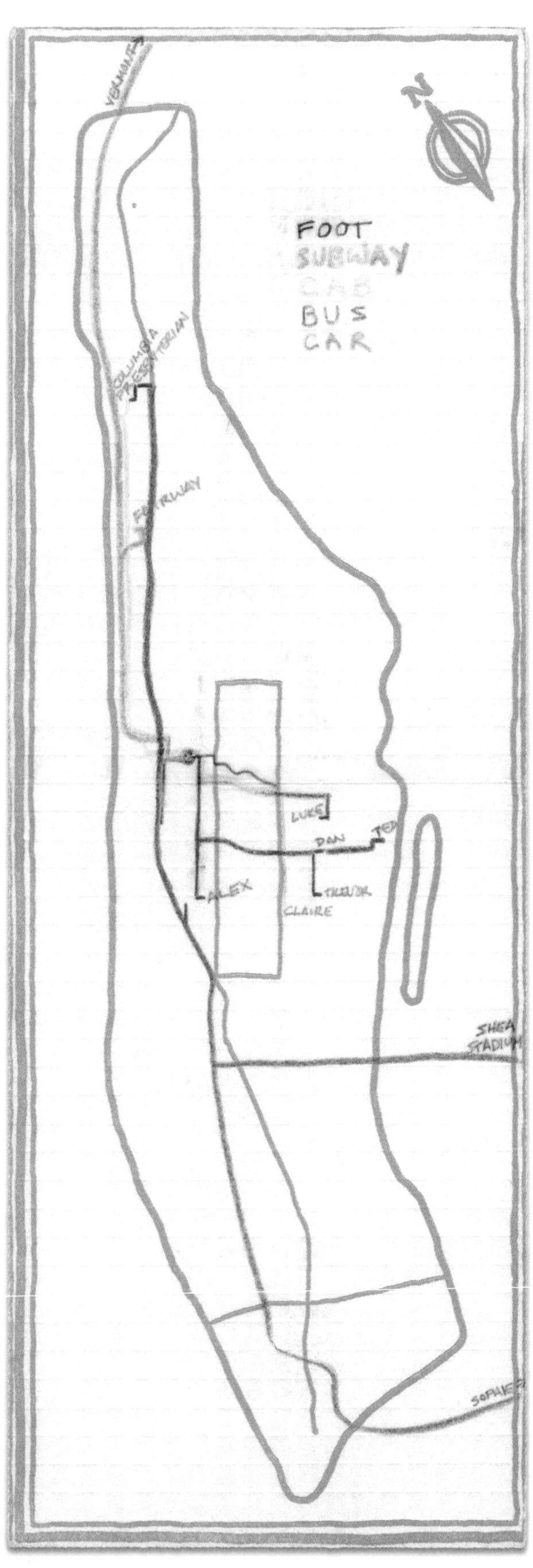
N
FOOT
SUBWAY
CAB
BUS
CAR
VERMONT
COLUMBIA PRESBYTERIAN
FAIRWAY
LUKE
DAN
TED
ALEX
TREVOR
CLAIRE
SHEA STADIUM
SOPHIE

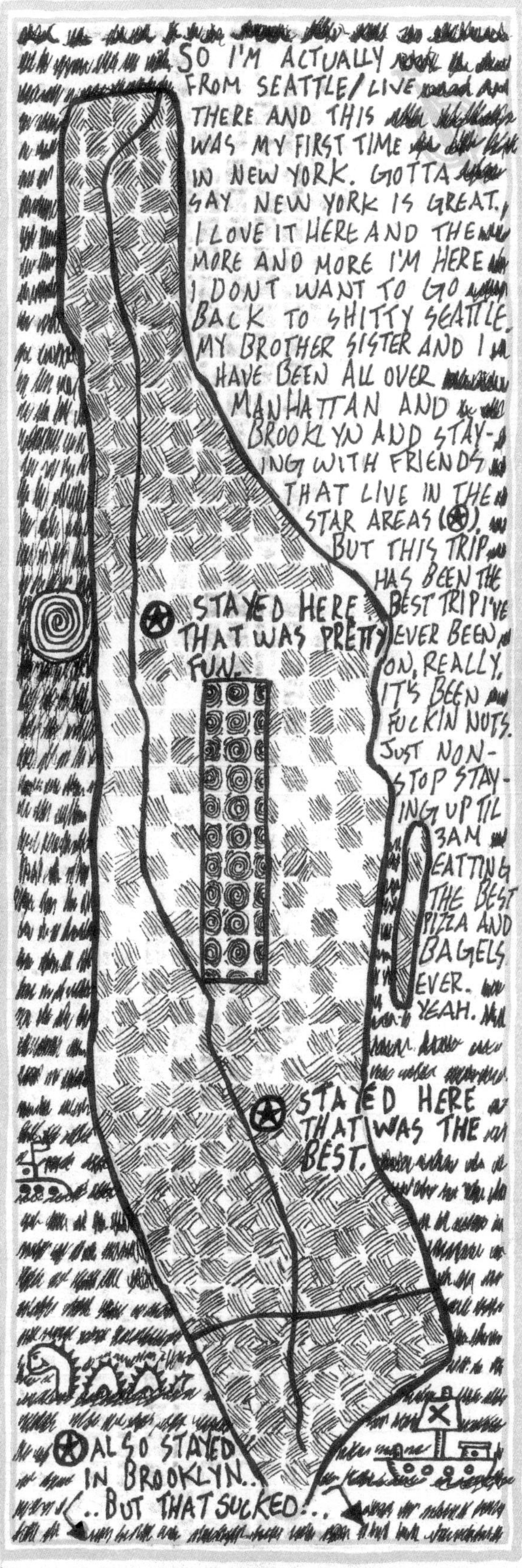
SO I'M ACTUALLY
FROM SEATTLE/LIVE
THERE AND THIS
WAS MY FIRST TIME
IN NEW YORK. GOTTA
SAY NEW YORK IS GREAT.
I LOVE IT HERE AND THE
MORE AND MORE I'M HERE
I DONT WANT TO GO
BACK TO SHITTY SEATTLE.
MY BROTHER SISTER AND I
HAVE BEEN ALL OVER
MANHATTAN AND
BROOKLYN AND STAY-
ING WITH FRIENDS
THAT LIVE IN THE
STAR AREAS (★).
BUT THIS TRIP
HAS BEEN THE
BEST TRIP I'VE
EVER BEEN
ON, REALLY.
IT'S BEEN
FUCKIN NUTS.
JUST NON-
STOP STAY-
ING UP TIL
3AM
EATTING
THE BEST
PIZZA AND
BAGELS
EVER.
YEAH.
STAYED HERE THAT WAS PRETTY FUN.
STAYED HERE THAT WAS THE BEST.
ALSO STAYED IN BROOKLYN..
..BUT THAT SUCKED!..

SEA-ATTLE

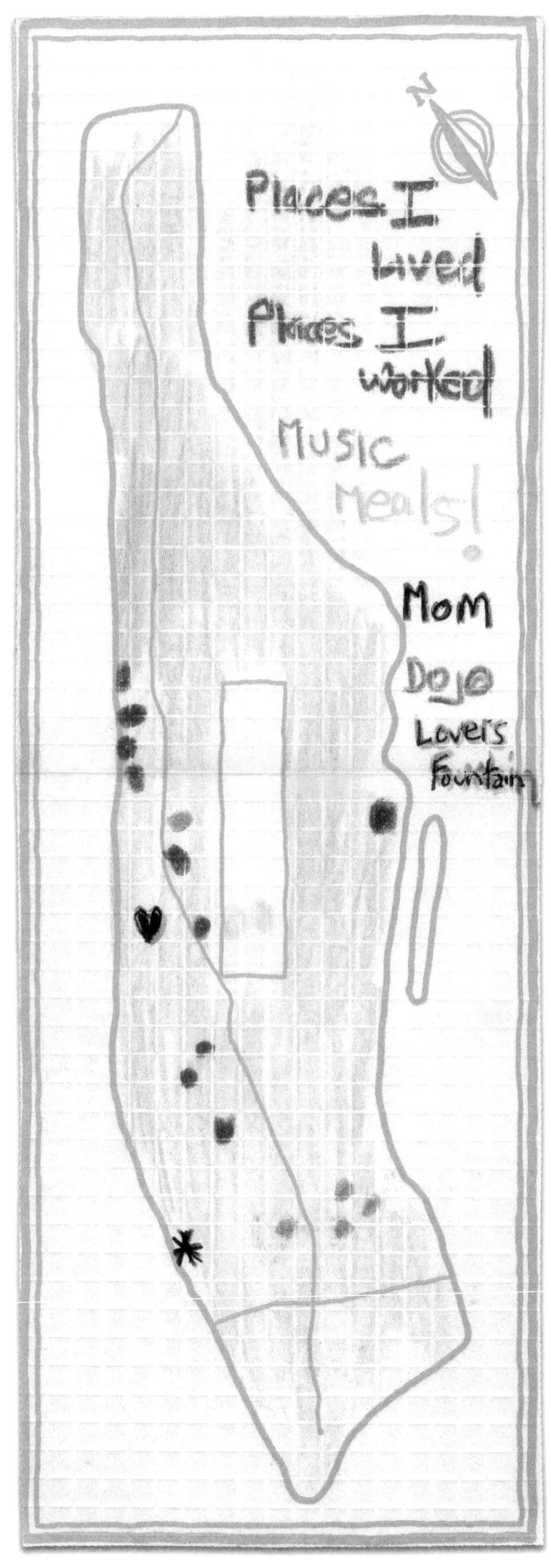
N
Places I
Lived
Places I
worked
Music
Meals!
Mom
Dojo
Lovers
Fountain

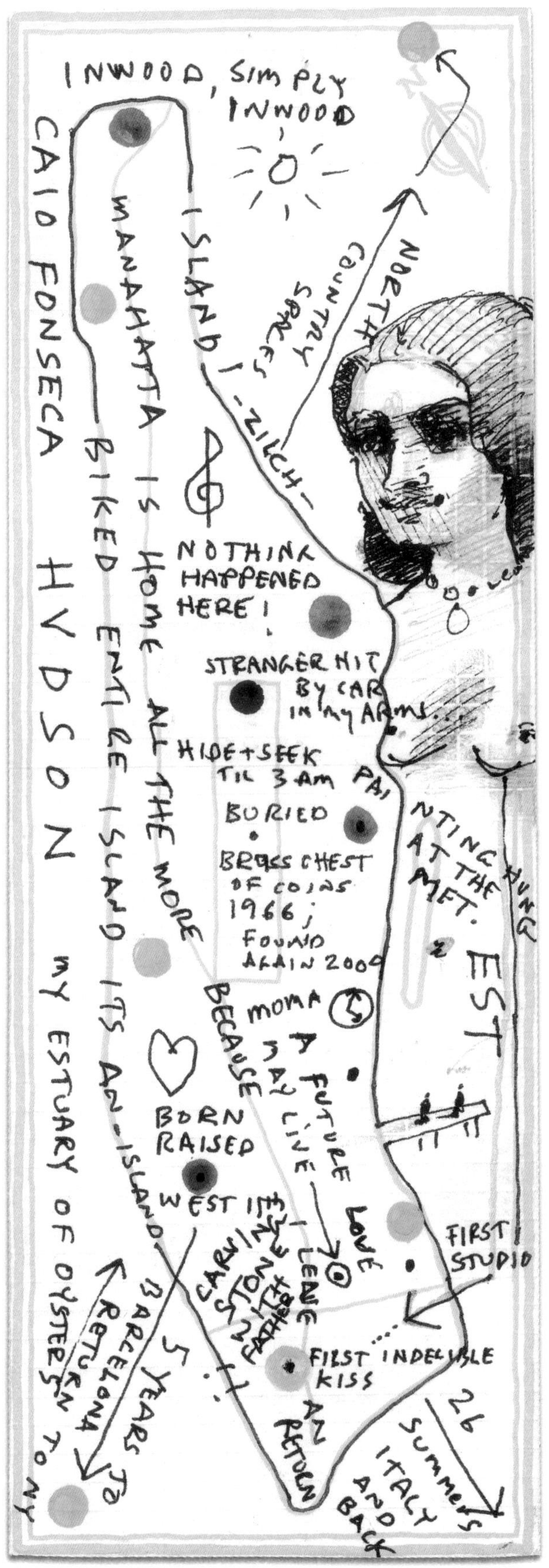
INWOOD, SIMPLY INWOOD
CAIO FONSECA
MANAHATTA IS HOME ALL THE MORE
ISLAND! -ZILCH-
NORTH COUNTRY SPACES
NOTHING HAPPENED HERE!
STRANGER HIT BY CAR IN MY ARMS...
HIDE+SEEK TIL 3 AM
BURIED BRASS CHEST OF COINS 1966; FOUND AGAIN 2004
PAINTING HUNG AT THE MET.
HUDSON
BIKED ENTIRE ISLAND ITS AN-ISLAND
BECAUSE
MOMA
FUTURE
EST
BORN RAISED
WEST 11TH
FIRST STUDIO
LOVE
FIRST INDELIBLE KISS
AN RETURN
5 YEARS TO BARCELONA RETURN TO NY
MY ESTUARY OF OYSTERS
26 SUMMERS ITALY AND BACK

175TH STREET—UNITED PALACE CATHEDRAL, 12:20 P.M. It's nearing the end of the second hour, and the noon sun is passing over us. ■ Ama and I are just beyond Inwood Hill Park, where a man who looked like he could eat us said, "Have you seen a hummingbird from up close? But really. Its wings, its heart. I'll map that." ■ We hand three maps to the *Watchtower* ladies sitting on the edge of Fort Tryon Park. (In return for their accepting our maps, we take their reading material—two brochures, one on depression and the other entitled "Global Warming?") Ama hands maps to a pair of cops in front of the 34th Precinct who ask if they could map their homicide cases. And I hand a map to a woman tending a churros stand, trying to pass off my Italian for Spanish. *"Draw your mind"* is the phrase that finally gets her to take it. ■ We're now on 181st Street, walking in Washington and his men's Revolutionary War footsteps, just south of the ghost of Fort Washington and just north of one of Manhattan's rare lighthouses. ■ At 175th, I pause to take in the obsessively ornate United Palace Cathedral that occupies the whole block. It was built in 1930 to be a vaudeville theater—a cousin of the original Ziegfeld—but it quickly became a movie palace. Then in 1969, a time when most Manhattan movie palaces were being razed, Reverend Ike saved the cinema by transforming it into a church. ■ The palace still has all the details of the Loew's Wonder Theatre it once was: the gold and mint marquee, the ticket booth at the entrance. But the details have been repurposed. The marquee reads: *United Church. All Welcome. Bienvenidos Todos.* ■ *Come on in or smile as you pass,* another face of the marquee reads. Birds fly in unison away from its wedding-cake facade.

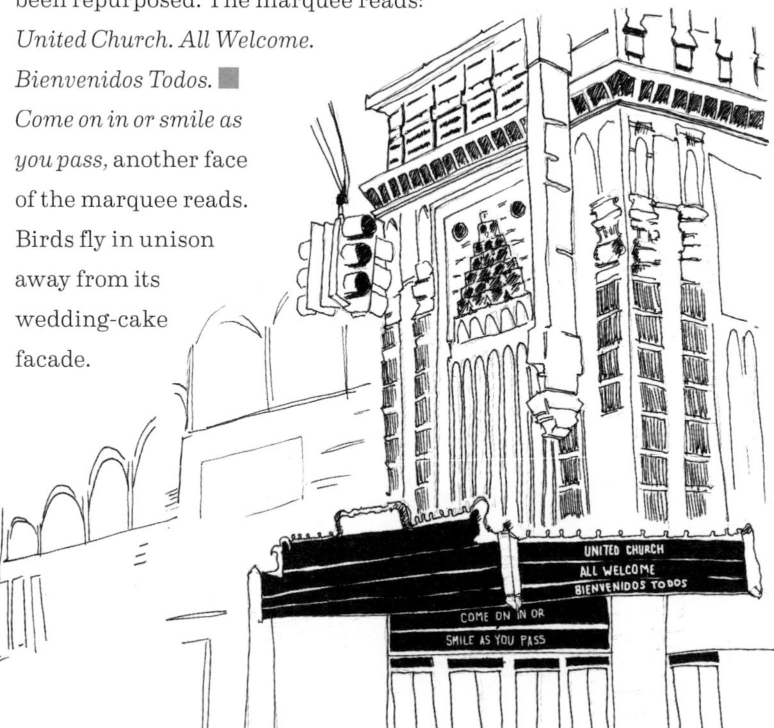

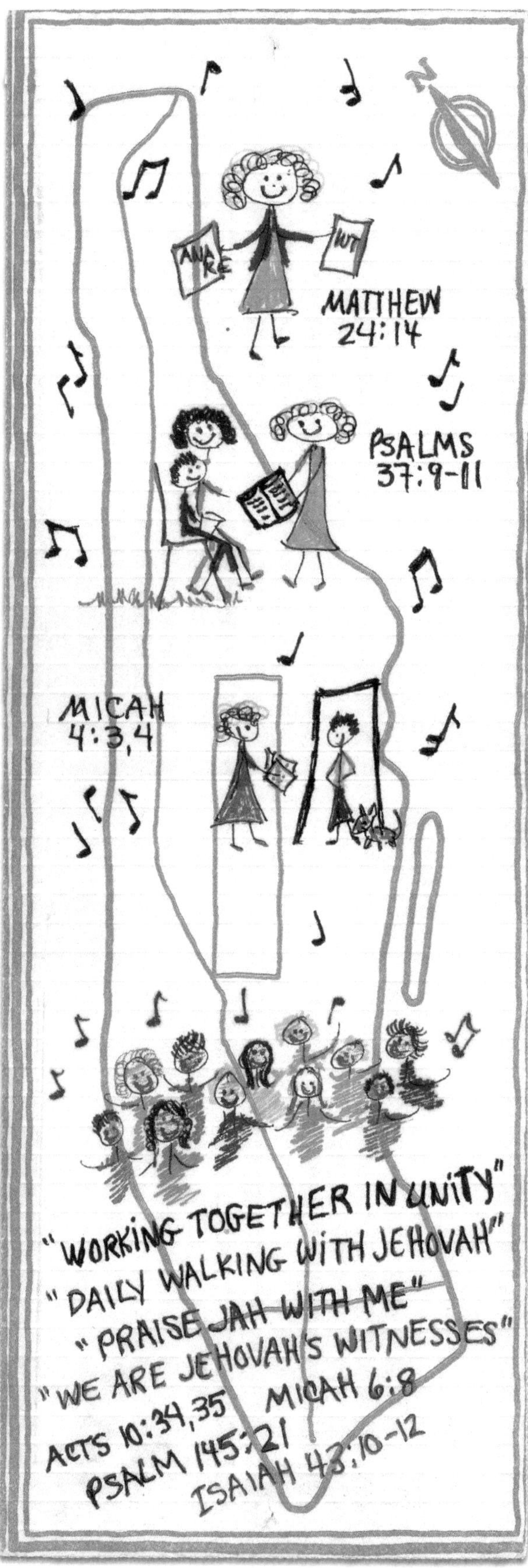
MATTHEW
24:14
PSALMS
37:9-11
MICAH
4:3,4
"WORKING TOGETHER IN UNITY"
"DAILY WALKING WITH JEHOVAH"
"PRAISE JAH WITH ME"
"WE ARE JEHOVAH'S WITNESSES"
ACTS 10:34,35
MICAH 6:8
PSALM 145:21
ISAIAH 43:10-12

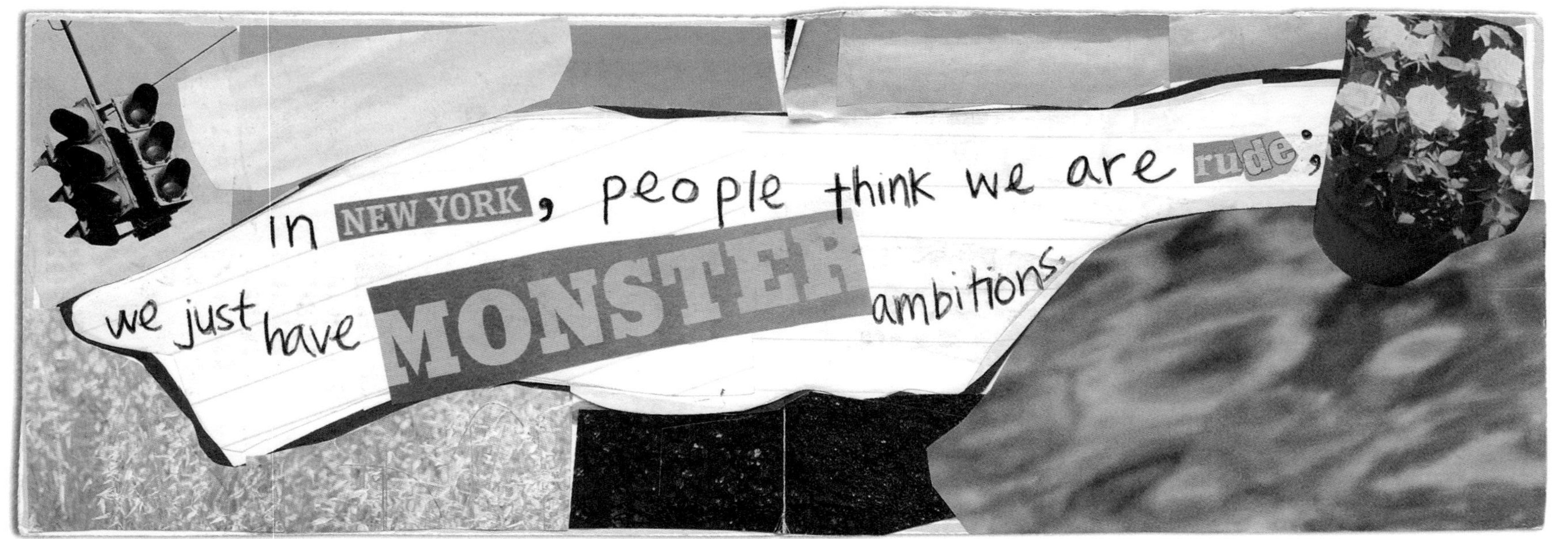
in NEW YORK, people think we are rude;
we just have MONSTER ambitions.

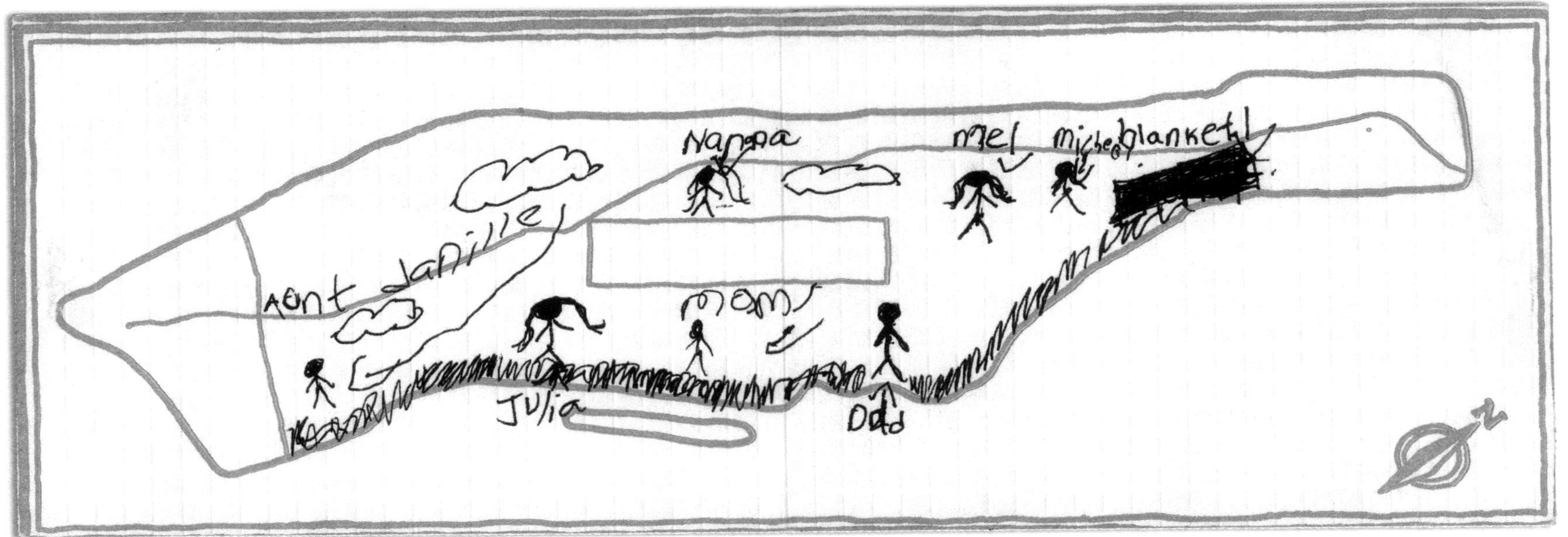
Aent Danille
Nappa
Mel
Micheal
blanket
Mom
Julia
Dad
N

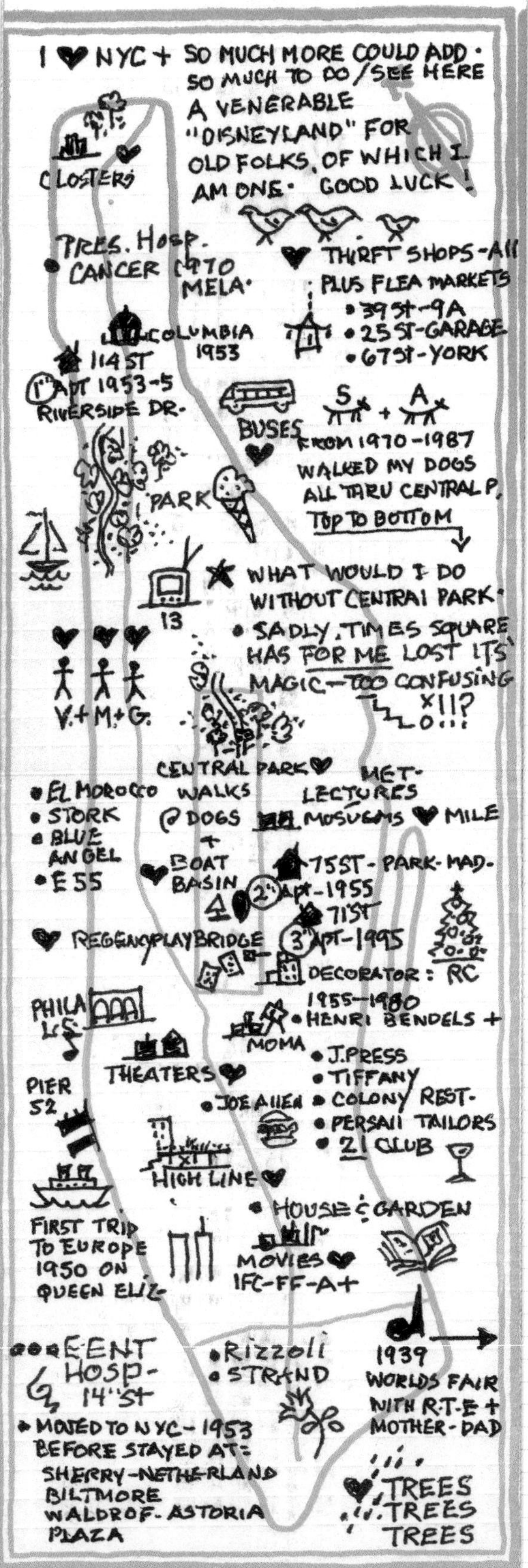
I ♥ NYC + SO MUCH MORE COULD ADD · SO MUCH TO DO / SEE HERE
A VENERABLE "DISNEYLAND" FOR OLD FOLKS, OF WHICH I AM ONE · GOOD LUCK!
CLOSTERS
PRES. HOSP. CANCER 1970 MELA·
♥ THRIFT SHOPS - ALL PLUS FLEA MARKETS
• 39 St - 9A
• 25 ST - GARAGE
• 67 St - YORK
COLUMBIA 1953
114 ST
1st APT 1953-5
RIVERSIDE DR.
S + A
BUSES
♥ FROM 1970-1987 WALKED MY DOGS ALL THRU CENTRAL P. TOP TO BOTTOM
PARK
13
★ WHAT WOULD I DO WITHOUT CENTRAL PARK ·
• SADLY, TIMES SQUARE HAS FOR ME LOST ITS MAGIC — TOO CONFUSING
V. + M. + G.
CENTRAL PARK ♥ WALKS @ DOGS +
MET - LECTURES MUSEUMS ♥ MILE
• EL MOROCCO
• STORK
• BLUE ANGEL
• E 55
♥ BOAT BASIN
75 ST - PARK - MAD - 2nd APT - 1955
71 ST 3rd APT - 1995
♥ REGENCY PLAY BRIDGE
DECORATOR: RC 1955-1980
• HENRI BENDELS +
PHILA
MOMA
THEATERS ♥
• J. PRESS
• TIFFANY
• COLONY REST.
• PERSAII TAILORS
• 21 CLUB
PIER 52
• JOE ALLEN
HIGH LINE ♥
• HOUSE & GARDEN
FIRST TRIP TO EUROPE 1950 ON QUEEN ELIZ.
MOVIES ♥ IFC - FF - A +
EENT HOSP - 14th St
• RIZZOLI
• STRAND
1939 WORLDS FAIR WITH R.T.E + MOTHER - DAD
• MOVED TO NYC - 1953 BEFORE STAYED AT:
SHERRY - NETHERLAND
BILTMORE
WALDROF - ASTORIA
PLAZA
♥ TREES TREES TREES

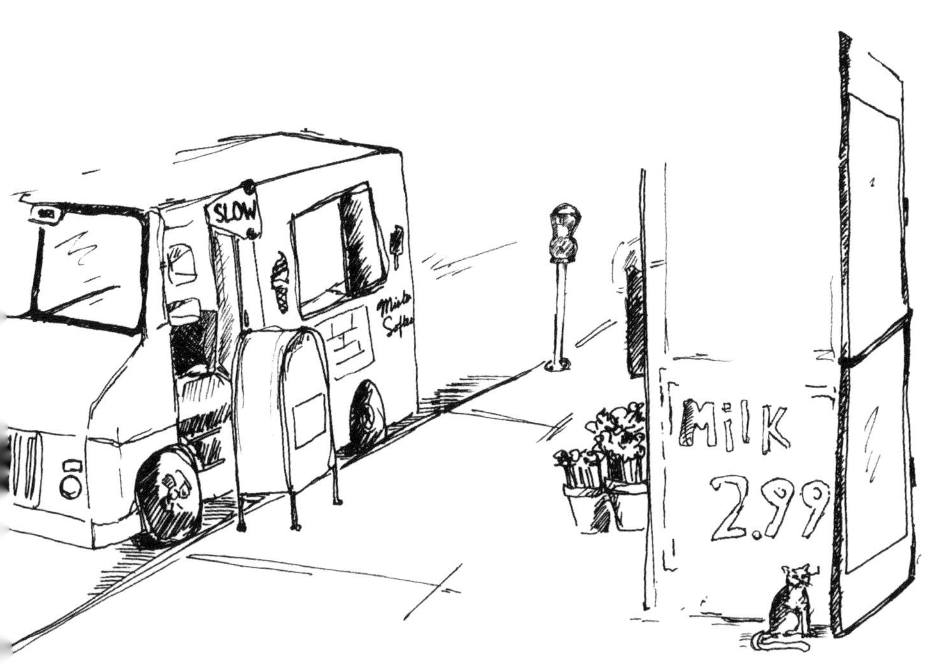

You caught me off guard on Central Park Mall—normally I would have smiled a "no thank you"—but when I started your request I was filled with so many thoughts of yesteryear that I couldn't believe I'd been here that long—many places have gone, and with them many recollections at least I hope so—but there were good times too. ■ New York is such [a] vast conglomerate, no wonder everybody (except my brother!) wants to get a taste of it. All the very best in your project. —One of many ■ P.S. Of course, I've not mentioned the places, as I've said, I'd soon forget—like most everyone I've been high, and God knows I have had my low times here too. But right now as an old person I couldn't be happier. My advice to any young person that's not too happy is just stay in there. We have such an extraordinary gift of just being here—think about it—and I don't mean New York alone—I mean living on this planet. ■ I'm going on too long. Thank God there's no more room. Good luck!

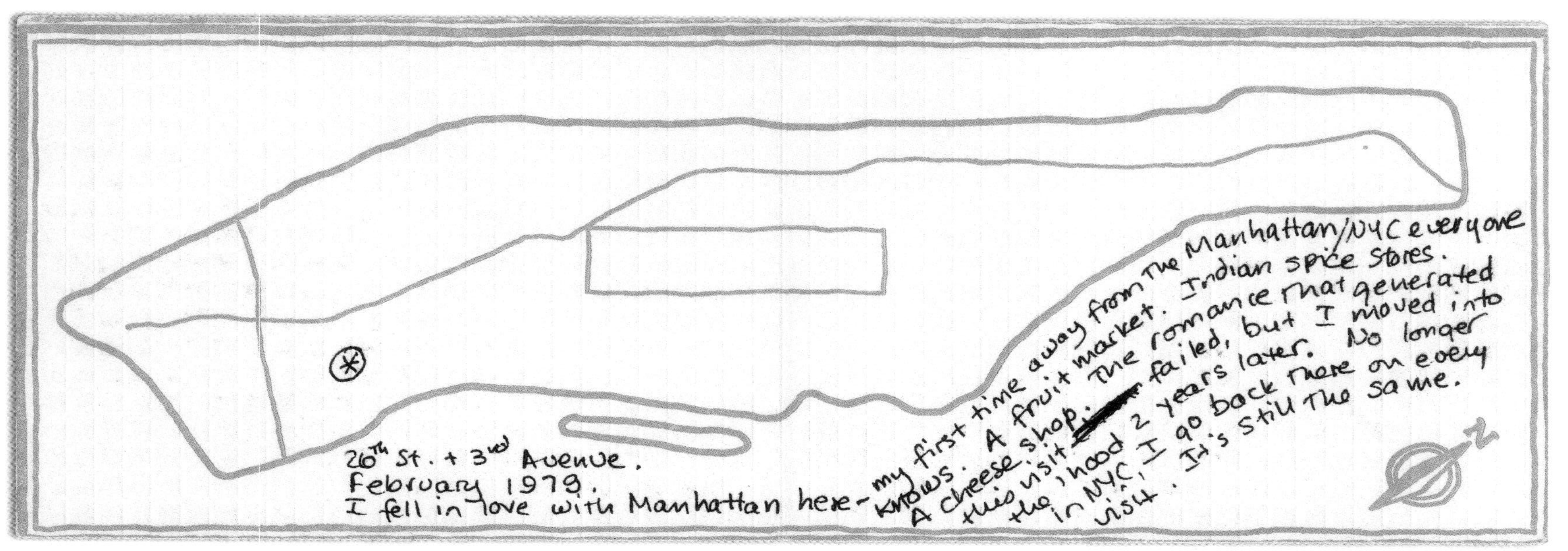
26th St. + 3rd Avenue.
February 1979.
I fell in love with Manhattan here—my first time away from the Manhattan/NYC everyone knows. A fruit market. Indian spice stores. A cheese shop. The romance that generated this visit failed, but I moved into the hood 2 years later. No longer in NYC, I go back there on every visit. It's still the same.
N

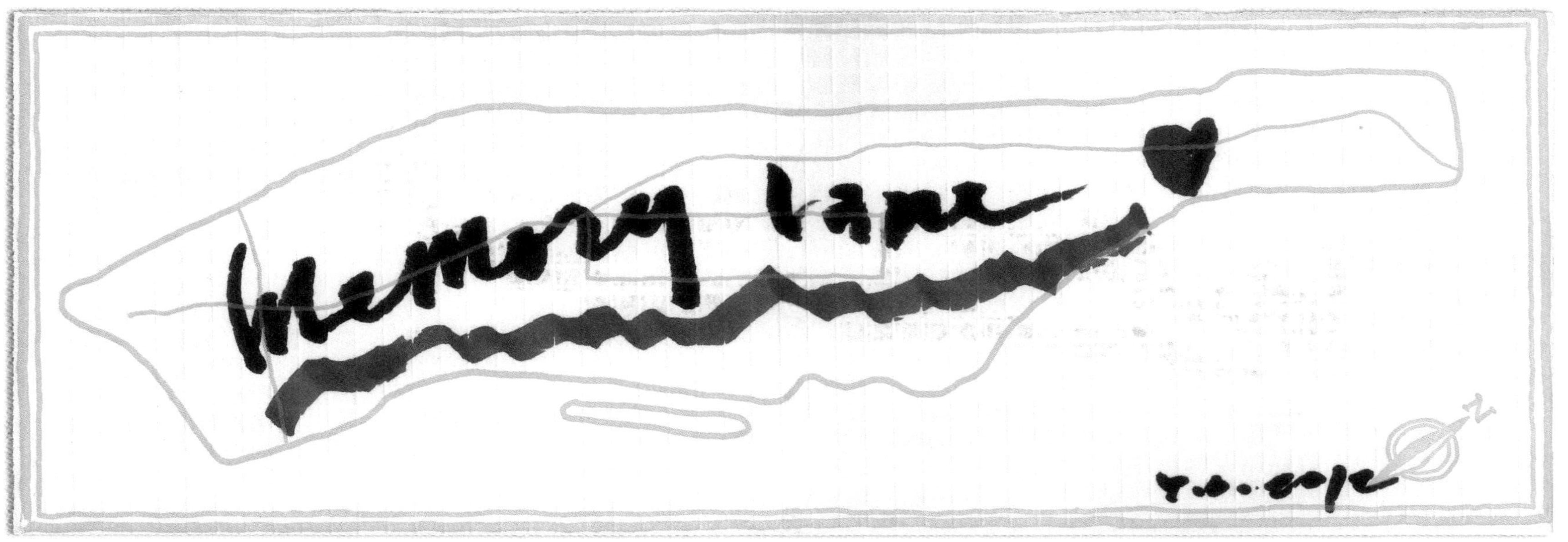
memory lane

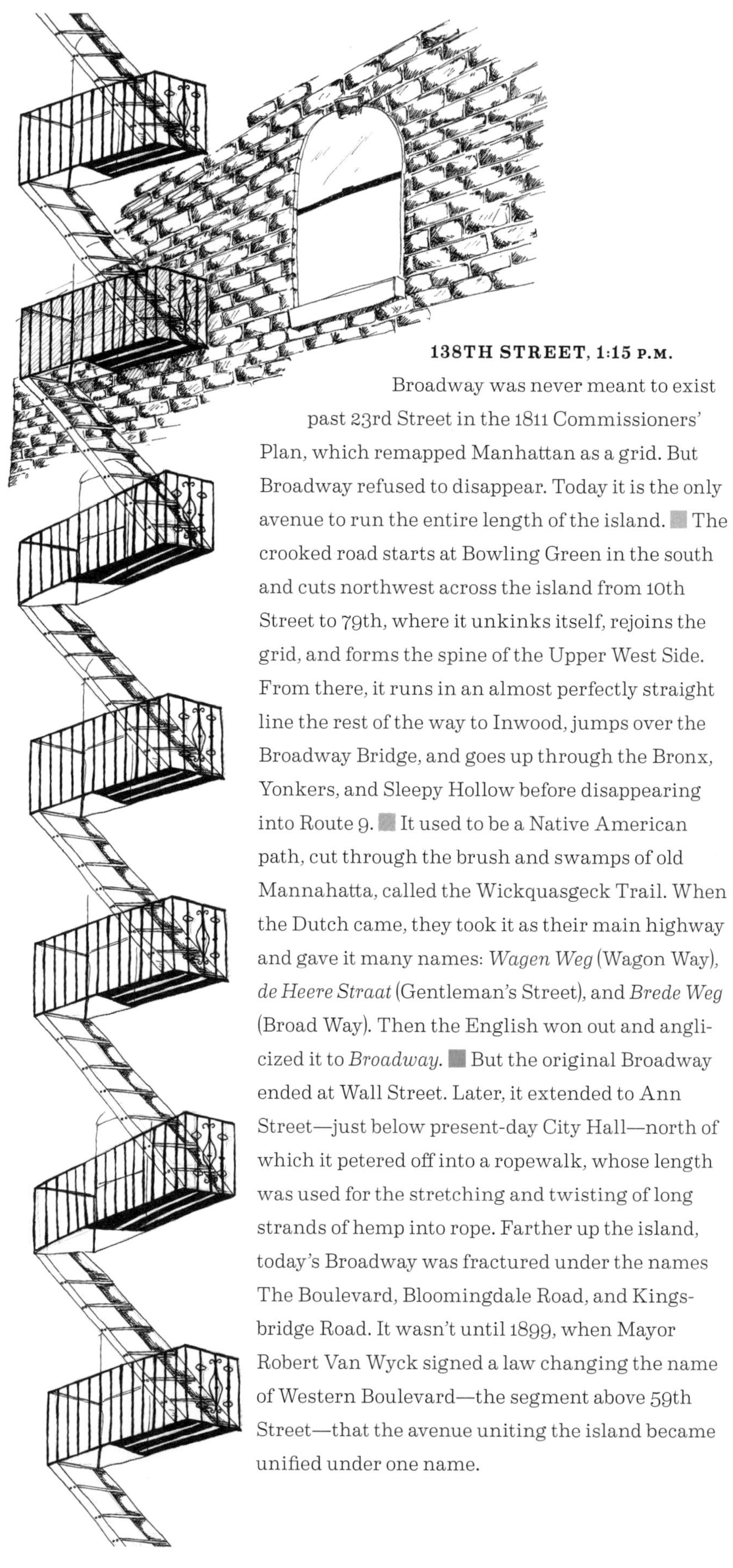

138TH STREET, 1:15 P.M.

Broadway was never meant to exist past 23rd Street in the 1811 Commissioners' Plan, which remapped Manhattan as a grid. But Broadway refused to disappear. Today it is the only avenue to run the entire length of the island. ■ The crooked road starts at Bowling Green in the south and cuts northwest across the island from 10th Street to 79th, where it unkinks itself, rejoins the grid, and forms the spine of the Upper West Side. From there, it runs in an almost perfectly straight line the rest of the way to Inwood, jumps over the Broadway Bridge, and goes up through the Bronx, Yonkers, and Sleepy Hollow before disappearing into Route 9. ■ It used to be a Native American path, cut through the brush and swamps of old Mannahatta, called the Wickquasgeck Trail. When the Dutch came, they took it as their main highway and gave it many names: *Wagen Weg* (Wagon Way), *de Heere Straat* (Gentleman's Street), and *Brede Weg* (Broad Way). Then the English won out and anglicized it to *Broadway.* ■ But the original Broadway ended at Wall Street. Later, it extended to Ann Street—just below present-day City Hall—north of which it petered off into a ropewalk, whose length was used for the stretching and twisting of long strands of hemp into rope. Farther up the island, today's Broadway was fractured under the names The Boulevard, Bloomingdale Road, and Kingsbridge Road. It wasn't until 1899, when Mayor Robert Van Wyck signed a law changing the name of Western Boulevard—the segment above 59th Street—that the avenue uniting the island became unified under one name.

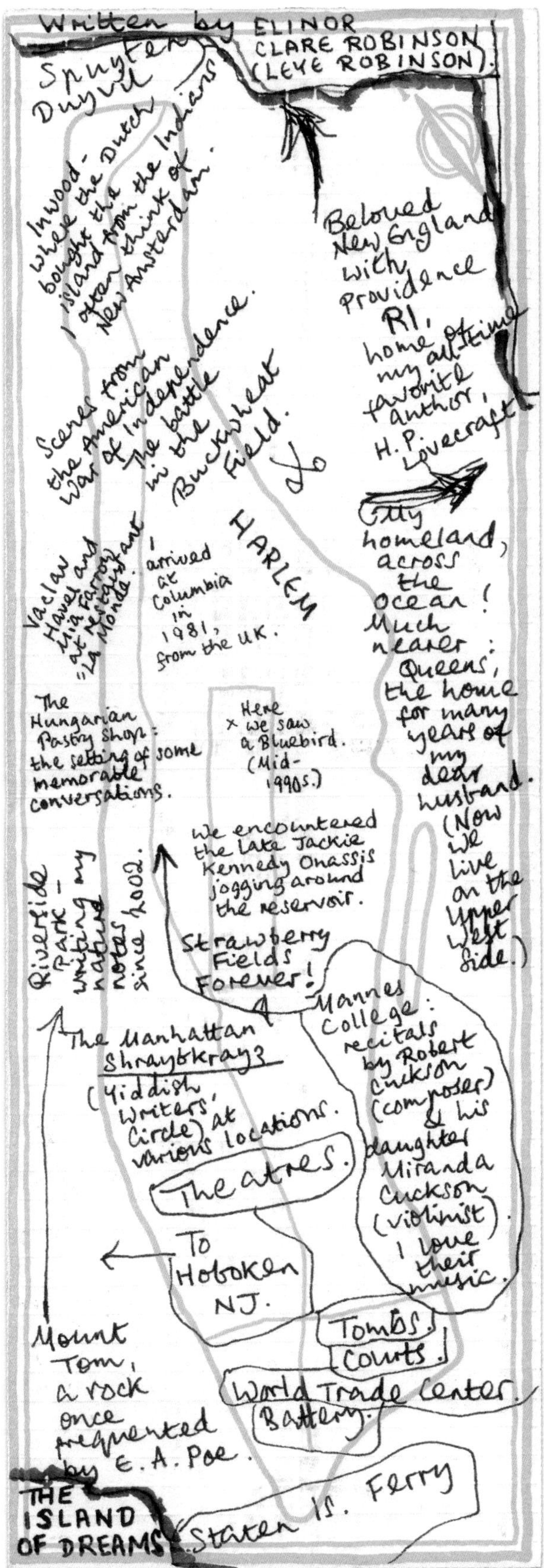
Written by ELINOR
CLARE ROBINSON
(LEYE ROBINSON)
Spuyten Duyvil
Inwood - where the Dutch bought the island from the Indians
often think of New Amsterdam.
Beloved New England with Providence RI, home of my all-time favorite author, H.P. Lovecraft
Scenes from the American War of Independence. The battle in the Buckwheat Field.
My homeland, across the ocean! Much nearer Queens, the home for many years of my dear husband. (Now we live on the Upper West Side.)
HARLEM
Vaclav Havel and Mia Farrow at restaurant "La Monde".
I arrived at Columbia in 1981, from the UK.
The Hungarian Pastry Shop: the setting of some memorable conversations.
Here we saw a Bluebird. (Mid-1990s.)
We encountered the late Jackie Kennedy Onassis jogging around the reservoir.
Riverside Park - writing my nature notes since 2002.
Strawberry Fields Forever!
Mannes College: recitals by Robert Cuckson (composer) & his daughter Miranda Cuckson (violinist). I love their music.
The Manhattan Shraybkrayz (Yiddish Writers' Circle) at various locations.
Theatres.
To Hoboken NJ.
Tombs.
Courts.
World Trade Center.
Battery.
Mount Tom, a rock once frequented by E. A. Poe.
Staten Is. Ferry
THE ISLAND OF DREAMS

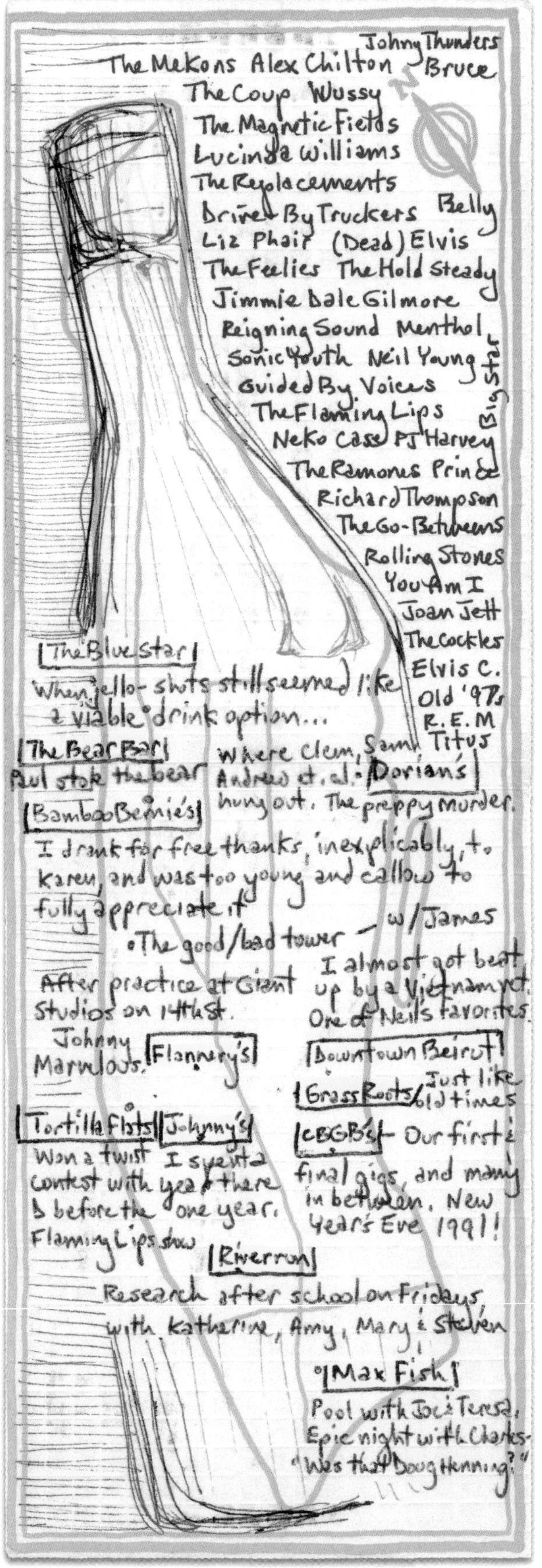
Johny Thunders
The Mekons Alex Chilton
Bruce
The Coup Wussy
The Magnetic Fields
Lucinda Williams
The Replacements
Drive By Truckers Belly
Liz Phair (Dead) Elvis
The Feelies The Hold Steady
Jimmie Dale Gilmore
Reigning Sound Menthol
Sonic Youth Neil Young
Guided By Voices
The Flaming Lips
Neko Case PJ Harvey
Big Star
The Ramones Prince
Richard Thompson
The Go-Betweens
Rolling Stones
You Am I
Joan Jett
The Cockles
Elvis C.
Old '97s
R.E.M
Titus
The Blue Star
When jello-shots still seemed like a viable drink option...
The Bear Bar
Paul stole the bear
Where Clem, Sam, Andrew et. al. hung out. The preppy murder.
Dorian's
Bamboo Bernie's
I drank for free thanks, inexplicably, to Karen, and was too young and callow to fully appreciate it
The good/bad tower — w/James
After practice at Giant Studios on 14th St.
I almost got beat up by a Vietnam vet. One of Neil's favorites.
Johnny Marvelous.
Flannery's
Downtown Beirut
Grass Roots
Just like old times
Tortilla Flats
Johnny's
CBGB's
Won a twist contest with yea & there b before the Flaming Lips show
I spent a year there one year.
Our first & final gigs, and many in between. New Year's Eve 1991!
Riverrun
Research after school on Fridays with Katherine, Amy, Mary & Stephen
Max Fish
Pool with Joe & Teresa, Epic night with Charles — "Was that Doug Henning?"

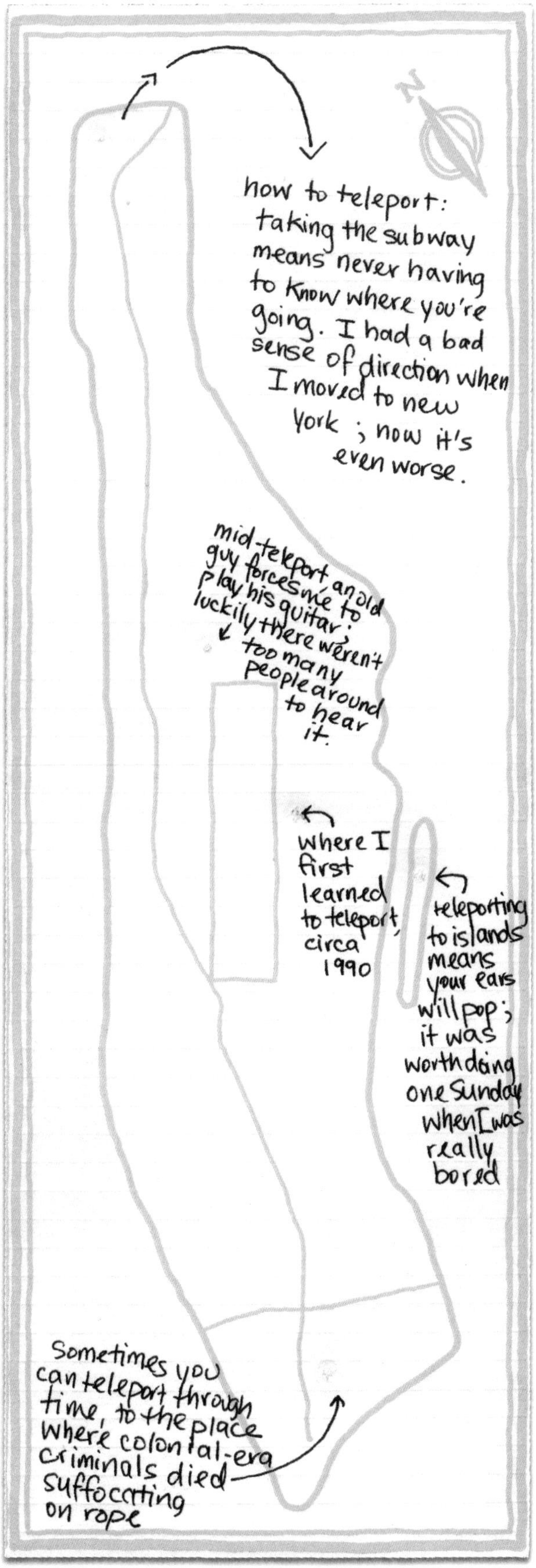

how to teleport:
taking the subway
means never having
to know where you're
going. I had a bad
sense of direction when
I moved to new
york ; now it's
even worse.

mid-teleport an old
guy forces me to
play his guitar;
luckily there weren't
too many
people around
to hear
it.

where I
first
learned
to teleport,
circa
1990

teleporting
to islands
means
your ears
will pop;
it was
worth doing
one Sunday
when I was
really
bored

Sometimes you
can teleport through
time, to the place
where colonial-era
criminals died
suffocating
on rope

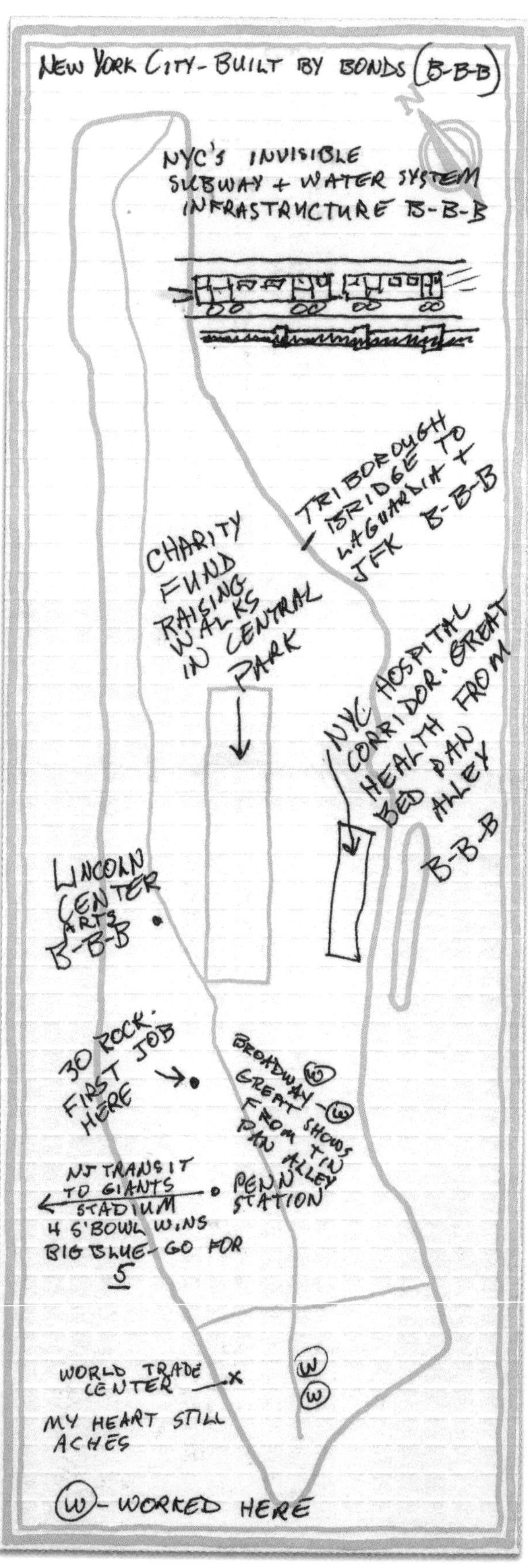
NEW YORK CITY - BUILT BY BONDS (B-B-B)
N
NYC'S INVISIBLE SUBWAY + WATER SYSTEM INFRASTRUCTURE B-B-B
TRIBOROUGH BRIDGE TO LAGUARDIA + JFK B-B-B
CHARITY FUND RAISING WALKS IN CENTRAL PARK
NYC HOSPITAL CORRIDOR. GREAT HEALTH FROM BED PAN ALLEY
B-B-B
LINCOLN CENTER ARTS B-B-B
30 ROCK: FIRST JOB HERE
BROADWAY - GREAT SHOWS FROM TIN PAN ALLEY
NJ TRANSIT TO GIANTS STADIUM
PENN STATION
4 S'BOWL WINS BIG BLUE - GO FOR 5
WORLD TRADE CENTER
MY HEART STILL ACHES
W - WORKED HERE

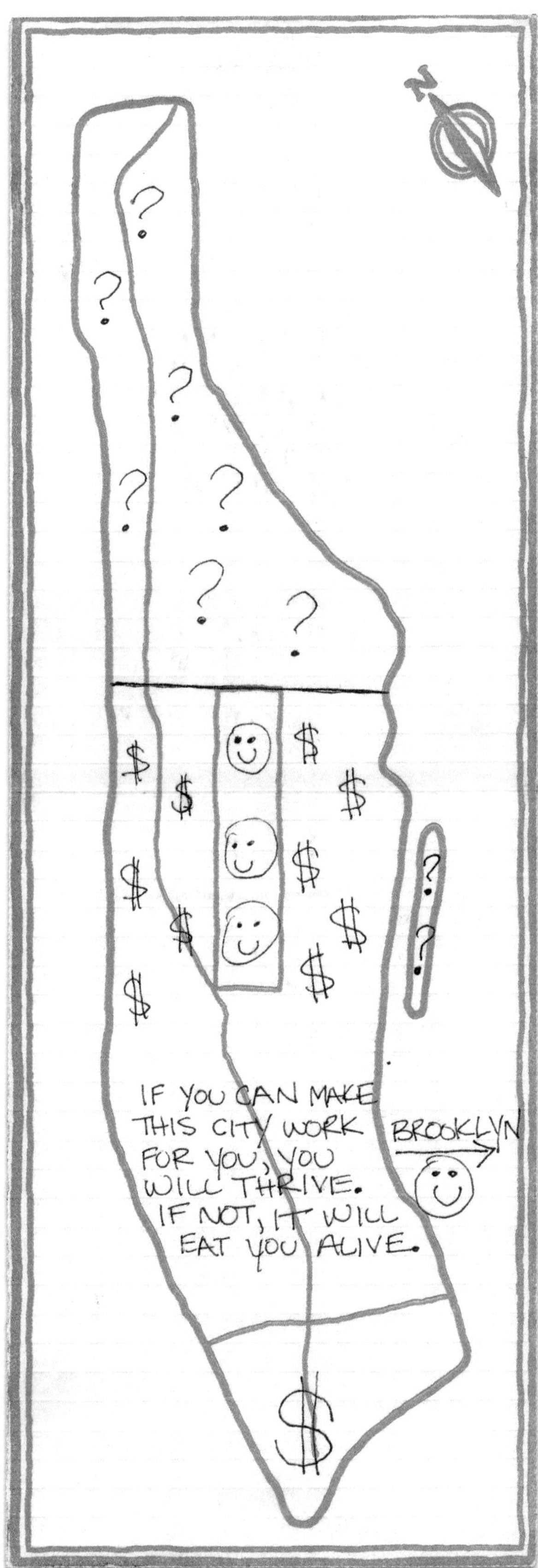
N
IF YOU CAN MAKE
THIS CITY WORK
FOR YOU, YOU
WILL THRIVE.
IF NOT, IT WILL
EAT YOU ALIVE.
BROOKLYN

112TH STREET—TOM'S RESTAURANT, 1:45 P.M.

The yucca of the bodegas is replaced by the no-spray lavender and bok choy of the sidewalk farmers' market near the iron gates of Columbia's main entrance. The C-Towns and Diamond Pawn shops have morphed into buildings with neo-Gothic flair, and the yelps of the I.S. 195 Roberto Clemente basketball players are replaced by the silence of a girl studying under a magnolia tree. In front of Tom's Restaurant, chess players duke it out on folding chairs as Morningside Heights onlookers gather. ■ An elderly man, hunched over his empty shopping cart, shuffles uptown on Broadway. Ama and I both bet he'll say no. He looks up from his orthopedic shoes when I ask him to join the project. ■ "Map my memories? All my memories are from here for the last fifty years." ■ His thick Yiddish accent is what I imagine my father's grandparents had when they settled in the tenements on the Lower East Side. He lingers on the *r*'s. I wonder if his parents moved here before the war, when the area to the north and east was Jewish Harlem, or if he was around as East Harlem shifted from an Italian neighborhood into El Barrio. I wonder what he thinks of the Whole Foods that opened a few blocks away. Or of the mannequins in mesh underwear bent over in the window of American Apparel just down the street. ■ He takes a map. "This is all I know. Is that okay?"

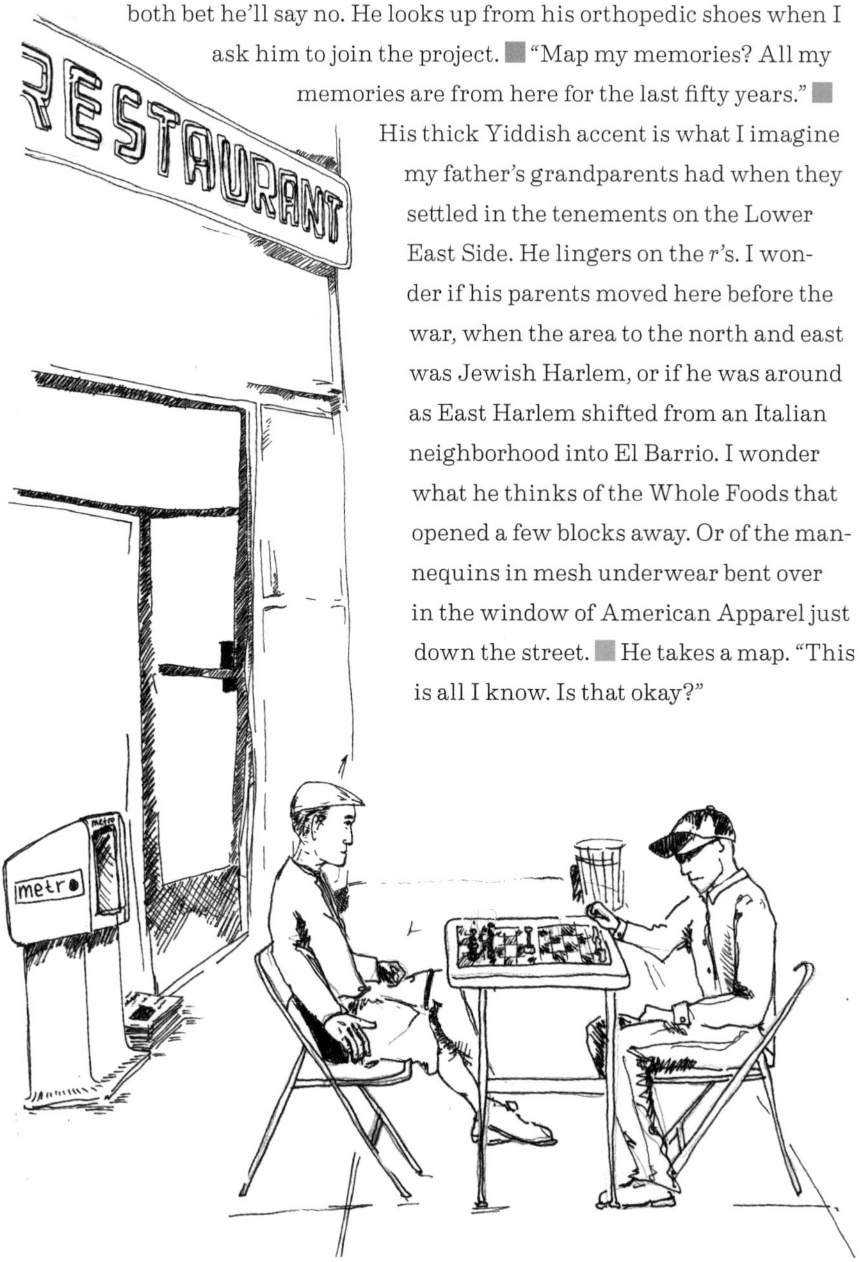

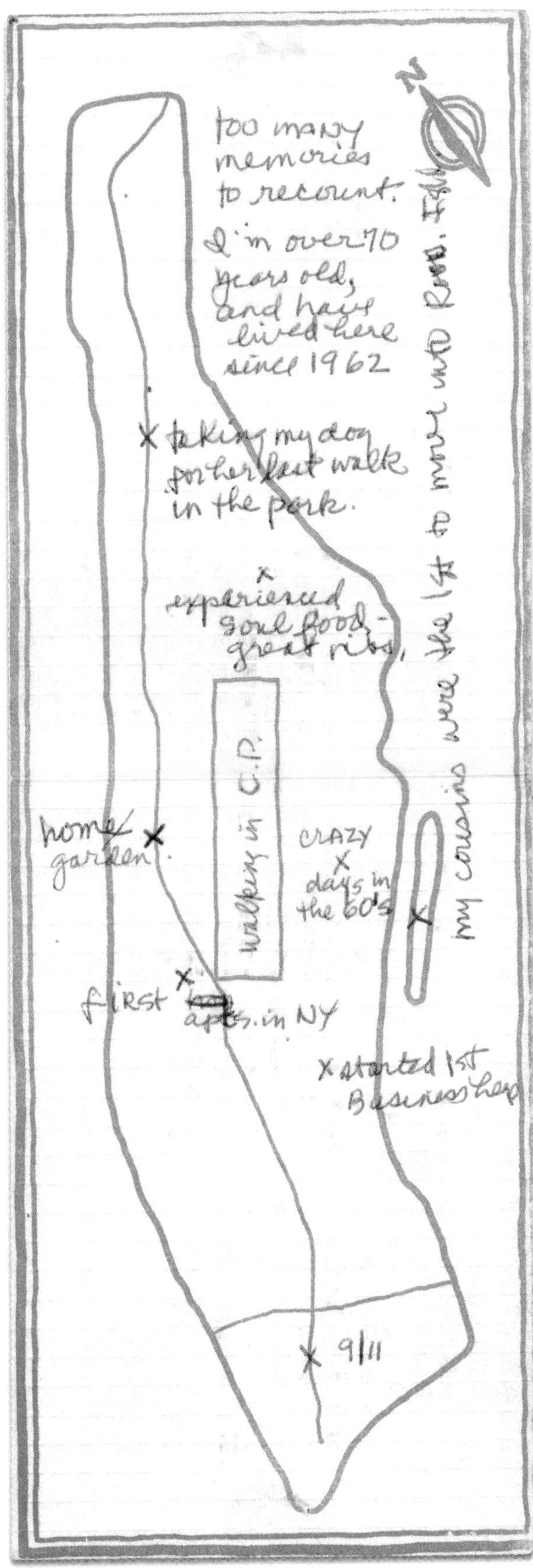
N
too many memories to recount.
I'm over 70 years old, and have lived here since 1962
my cousins were the 1st to move into Roos. Isl.
taking my dog for her last walk in the park.
experienced soul food - great ribs.
walking in C.P.
home/garden
CRAZY days in the 60's
first apts. in NY
started 1st Business here
9/11

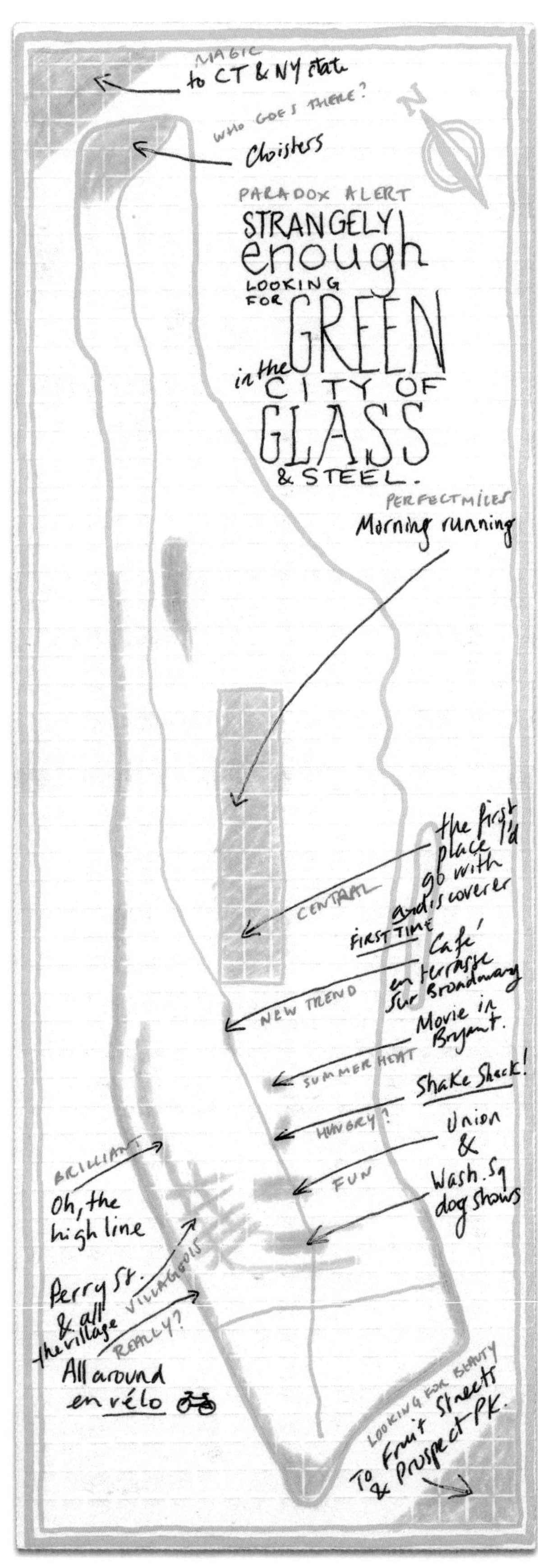
MAGIC
to CT & NY state
WHO GOES THERE?
Cloisters
PARADOX ALERT
STRANGELY enough LOOKING FOR GREEN in the CITY OF GLASS & STEEL.
PERFECT MILES
Morning running
the first place I'd go with a rediscoverer
CENTRAL
FIRST TIME
Café en terrasse sur Broadway
NEW TREND
Movie in Bryant.
SUMMER HEAT
Shake Shack!
HUNGRY?
Union & Wash. Sq dog shows
FUN
BRILLIANT
Oh, the high line
Perry St. & all the village
VILLAGEOIS
REALLY?
All around en vélo
LOOKING FOR BEAUTY
To Fruit Streets & Prospect PK.

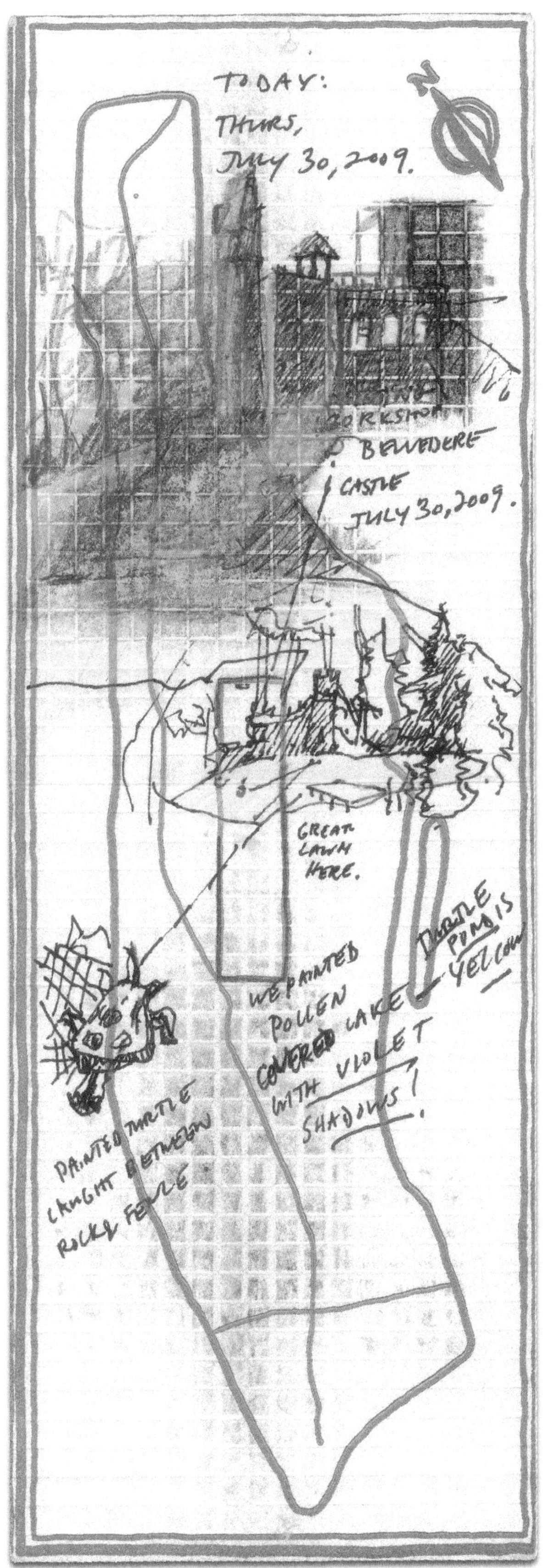
TODAY:
THURS,
JULY 30, 2009.
BELVEDERE
CASTLE
JULY 30, 2009.
GREAT
LAWN
HERE.
TURTLE
POND IS
WE PAINTED
POLLEN
COVERED LAKE
WITH VIOLET
SHADOWS!
PAINTED TURTLE
CAUGHT BETWEEN
ROCK & FENCE

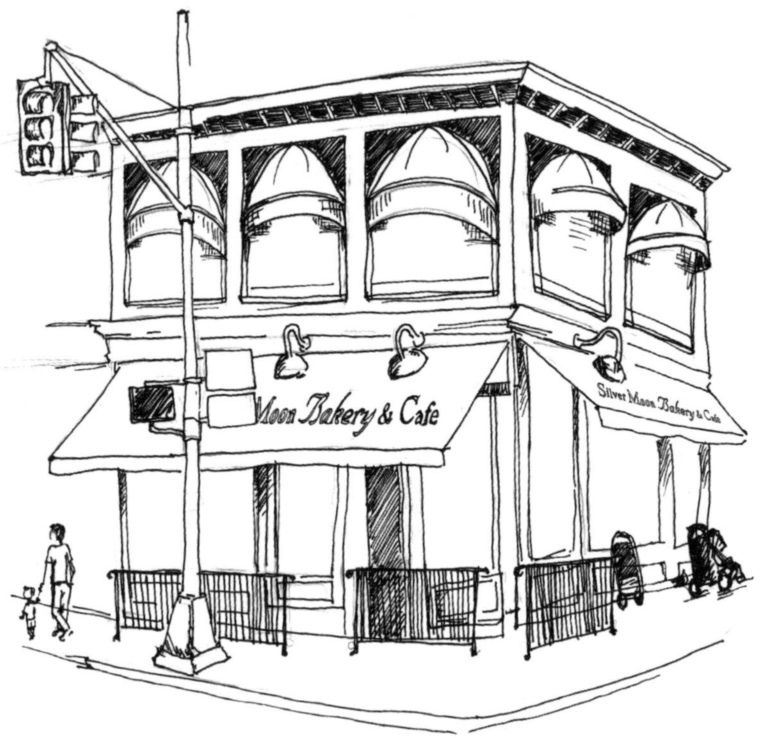

2740 BROADWAY, BETWEEN DUKE ELLINGTON BOULEVARD AND 105TH STREET—SILVER MOON BAKERY, 1:57 P.M.
Even after three hundred maps have been handed out, Ama and I still melt the moment people switch from being suspicious that we want to sell them something—"Heh? What do you want? Money? Directions?"—to realizing that we just want to know their stories, their memories, what they love—"Oh, in that case, thanks, sweeties!" ■ Ama and I stop for lunch at Absolute Bagels, the best bagel place in New York. It's run by a family of Thai immigrants who have mastered the double cooking technique (a bagel is first boiled, then baked) and harnessed New York's famous tap water to make perfect chewy, crunchy, toasted masterpieces. ■ Outside, crumpled shoulder bags, baseball hats, white hair, sneakers, and shopping carts flash by. An elderly woman on a scooter parallel parks next to a man also on a scooter. They lean over their handlebars to talk into each other's ear. A school bus of a stroller maneuvers around the chatterers. Construction workers share the bench in the middle of Broadway with college kids in skinny jeans and Ray-Bans, all eating sandwiches and drinking milky iced coffee. ■ Farther south, I slip three maps in quick succession through a McDonald's walk-through window, to the ticket vendor in Symphony Space's box office, and into the hands of a Mister Softee driver. ■ Manhattan feels as if it's passing by on a conveyor belt.

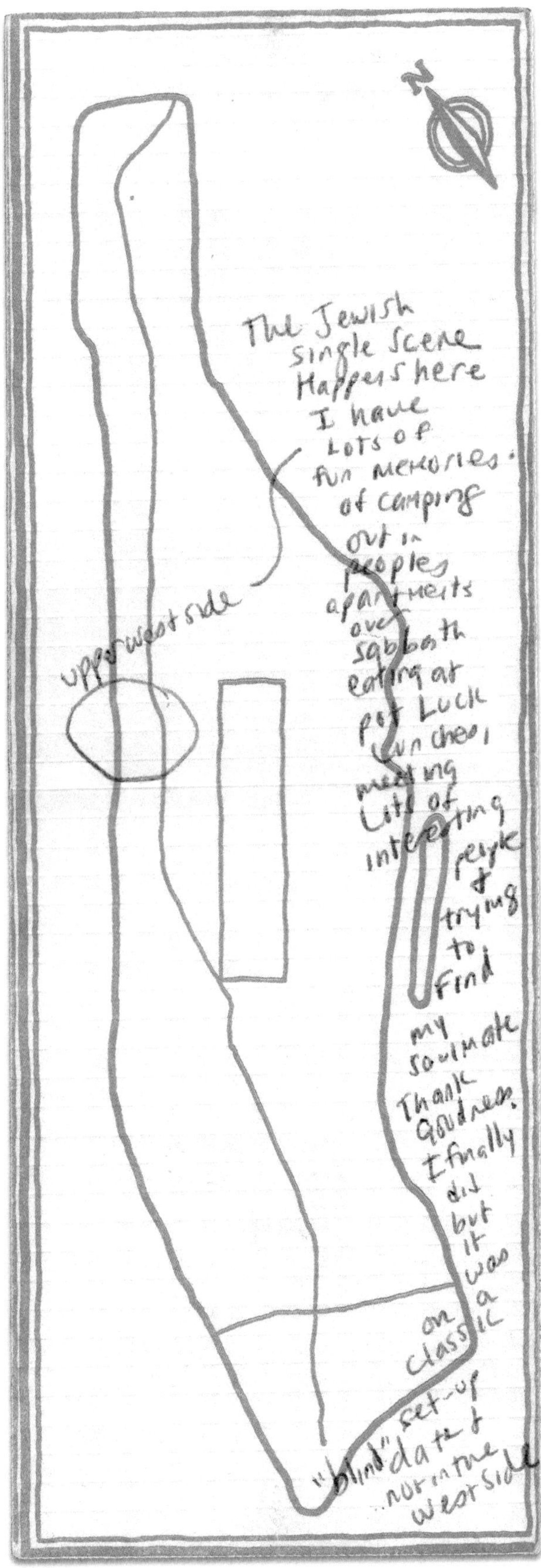
N
The Jewish
single scene
Happens here
I have
Lots of
fun memories
of camping
out in
peoples
apartments
over
Sabbath
eating at
pot Luck
luncheon,
meeting
Lots of
interesting
people
&
trying
to
Find
my
soulmate
Thank
goodness
I finally
did
but
it
was
a
classic
"blind" set-up
date &
not on the
west side
upper west side

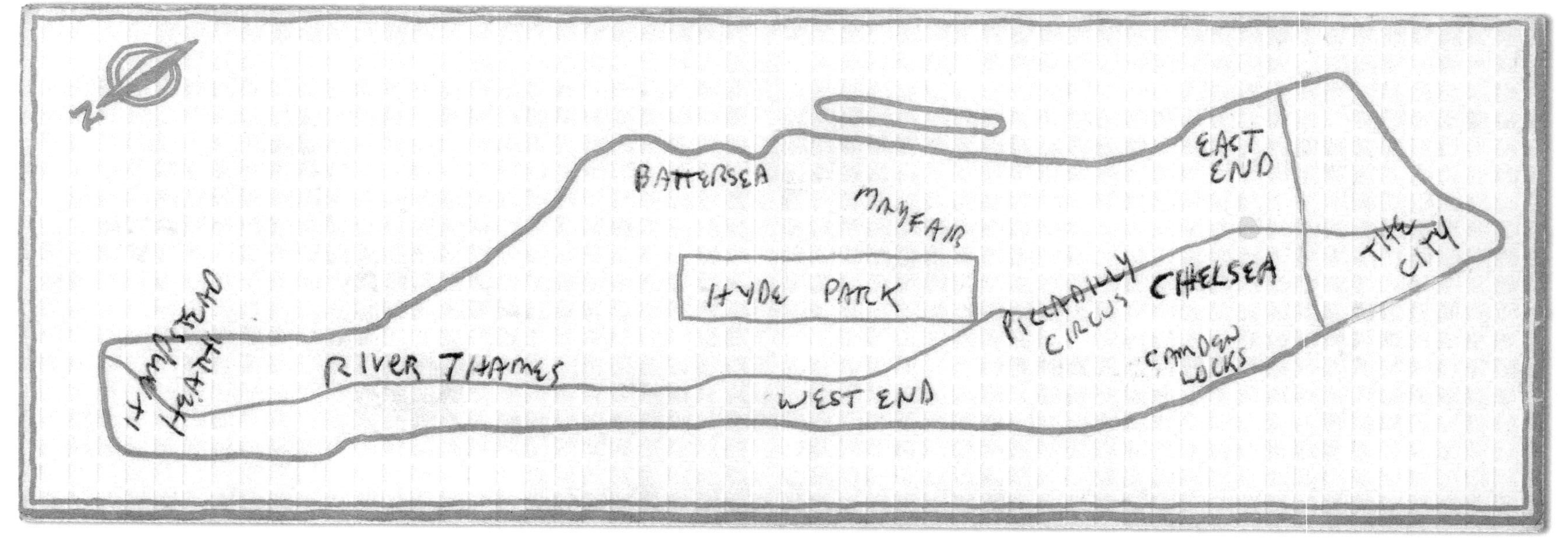
N
HAMPSTEAD HEATH
RIVER THAMES
BATTERSEA
MAYFAIR
HYDE PARK
WEST END
PICCADILLY CIRCUS
CHELSEA
CAMDEN LOCKS
EAST END
THE CITY

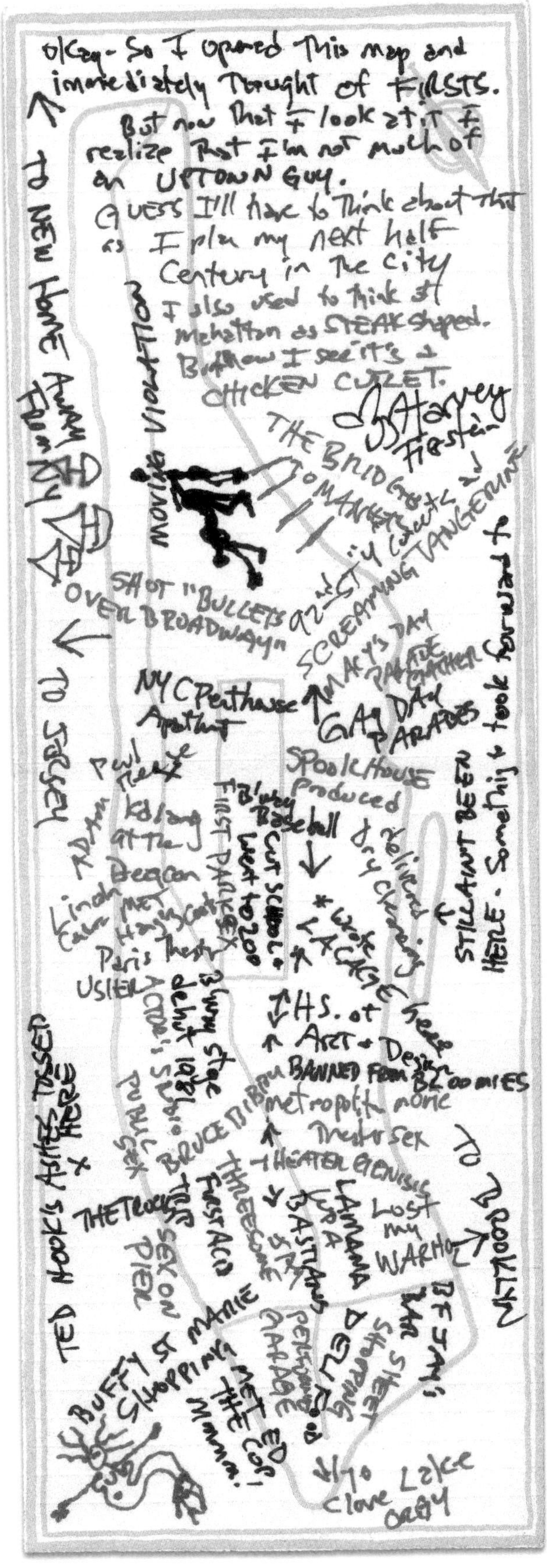

Okay- So I opened This map and immediately Thought of FIRSTS.
But now that I look at it I realize That I'm not much of an UPTOWN GUY.
GUESS I'll have to Think about that as I plan my next half Century in The City.
I also used to think of Manhattan as STEAK shaped.
But now I see it's a CHICKEN CUTLET.

Harvey Fierstein

TO NEW HOME AWAY FROM NY

MOVING VIOLATION

SCREAMING TANGERINE

SHOT "BULLETS OVER BROADWAY"

NYC Penthouse Apartment

MACY'S DAY PARADE

GAY DAY PARADES

SPOOKHOUSE Produced

TO JERSEY

STILL AIN'T BEEN HERE. Something to look forward to

Paris Theater USHER

H.S. of Art + Design

BANNED FROM BLOOMIES

TO BROOKLYN

Lost my WARHOL

SEX ON PIER

La MaMa

TO Lake Clove

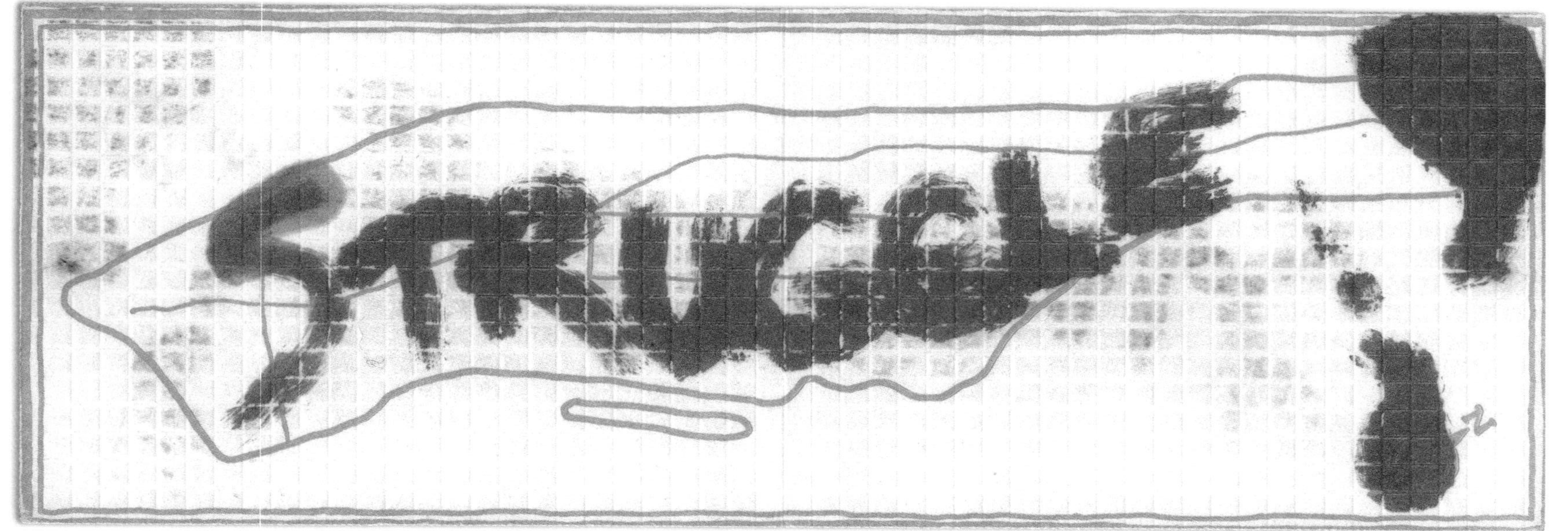
STRUGGLE
N

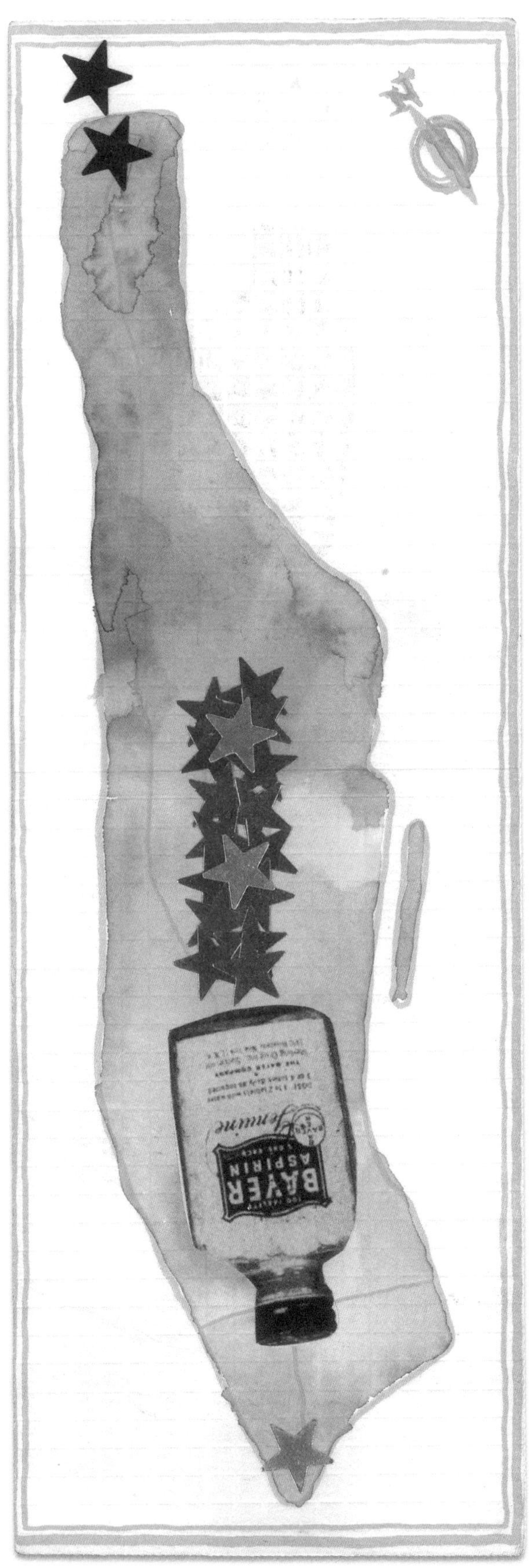
BAYER
ASPIRIN
Genuine

80TH STREET—ZABAR'S, 2:52 P.M.

For forty years, H&H Bagels and its sawdust-covered floor were located at the intersection of 80th Street and Broadway, until it closed in 2012. Four blocks from here, at what was the Brennan Farmhouse, it's rumored that Edgar Allan Poe wrote "The Raven." The house was destroyed after Poe's death, but the mantel sits quietly on the sixth-floor mezzanine of Columbia University's Butler Library. ■ Zabar's is getting ready for Passover: "Six pieces of gefilte fish"; "half-pound home-style red horseradish." Citarella, just down the street, is celebrating spring with a special on shad roe. A young violinist serenades the customers with "As Time Goes By." ■ Pat Flanagan, surveying the table vendors selling old books and wire jewelry, tells me of his adventures in the 1940s. "I just moved up to the Bronx, but for the first seventy years, this"—he gestures to Broadway—"this was it. It's *all* memories. Nights out drinking. Old lovers. Heartache. People think they know this area, but you see that grille?" ■ He waits until I follow the line of his pointing finger and face the street. ■ "People pass by this street every day, but they never notice the iron fence. It's got to be over a hundred years old. If the subway was built in 1904, and the grilles were there for ventilation from the very beginning . . . Well, let me tell you. Your project is about creativity, yes?" ■ I nod. ■ "Well, there's nothing more creative than a bunch of twelve-year-olds left to their own devices. I used to hang out there with the neighborhood boys and we would all go exploring. Those grilles are access points to the subway tunnels. And let. Me. Tell. You. It's like the nineteenth century down there. I'll map all of it for you. You'll be hearing from me, Becky."

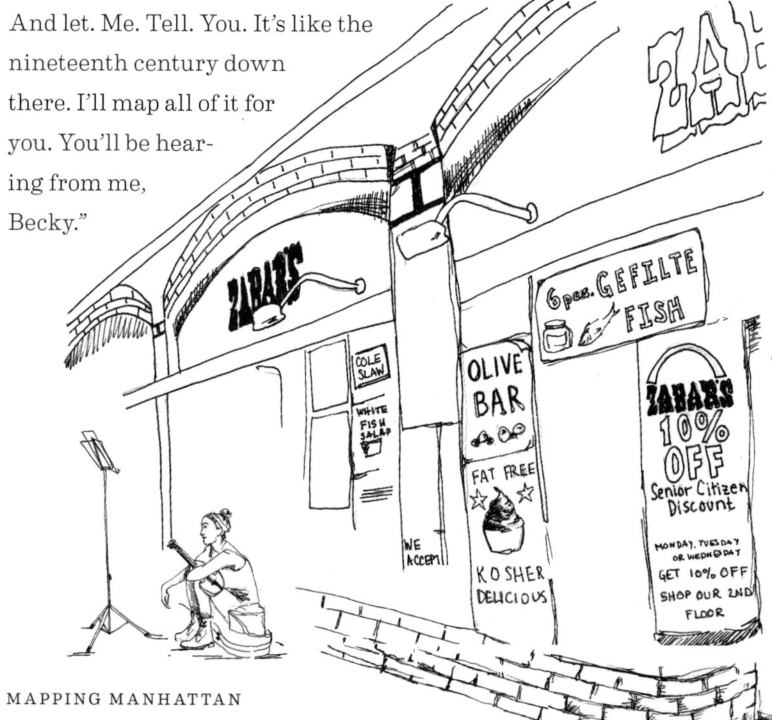

FLANAGAN, [illegible]

Bx, N.Y. [illegible]

Sept. 19 '09
8:42 P.M.

USA 28

Saturday night — the music songs & patter of the 20th c.
There's memories, mostly of Manhattan in the 2 hrs of play.
I've played with the shape of our island: is it like a leg of lamb, or maybe

My summer was a long series of events that seemed to happen with little planning. Even meeting you around 84th St. just because it was nice to stroll along in the sun. Where does our culture — our natural proximity to seasonal elements — cross paths? Columbus Circle? TIMES SQ.? Staten Is. Ferry? Pat

Rebecca Cooper
M.Y.M.
P.O. Box
356196
Briarwood, N.Y.
11435

more of a halved steer or a hook in a locker?
Anyhow, the shape — the actual island don't jibe.
B'way looks right. but where's the extension that is Battery Park City? And if I'm going to quibble, how about some of the other parks that may not be "castled" but have historical significance like Morningside behind Columbia, & steeply sloping down to Harlem.
Harlem, & the Dutch presence that goes back 400 yrs. Just now the celebration of Henry Hudson's discovery in the shadow of our national memorial to WTC/9-11-01.
I went from the bus stop at City Hall to St. Paul's Chapel & Graveyard, a landmark survivor from the 18th c.
We know what has happened; how about what will happen?
NOBODY EXPECTS THE UNEXPECTED. Pearl Harbor, earthquake, etc. Do you know there's a fault line across 125th St. There's also one in the Bronx. If S.F. can have them why

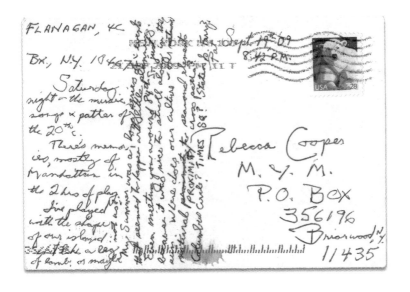

SEPTEMBER 19, 2009. 8:42 P.M.

Saturday night—the music, songs and patter of the 20th C. ■ There's memories, mostly of Manhattan in the 2 hrs of play. ■ I've played with the shape of our island: Is it like a leg of lamb, or maybe more of a halved steer or a hook in a locker? . . . ■ My summer was a long series of events that seemed to happen with little planning. Even meeting you around 84th Street, just because it was nice to stroll along in the sun. Where does our culture—our natural proximity to seasonal elements—cross paths? Columbus Circle? TIMES SQ.? Staten Is. Ferry? —Pat.

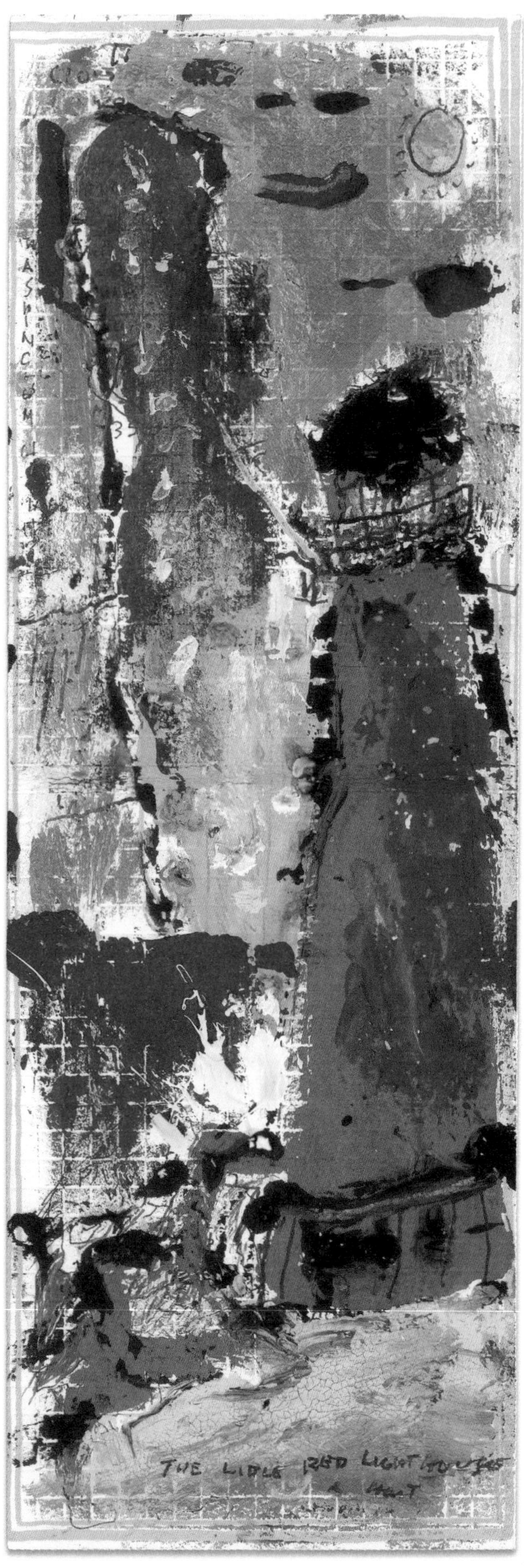
THE LIDLE RED LIGHT

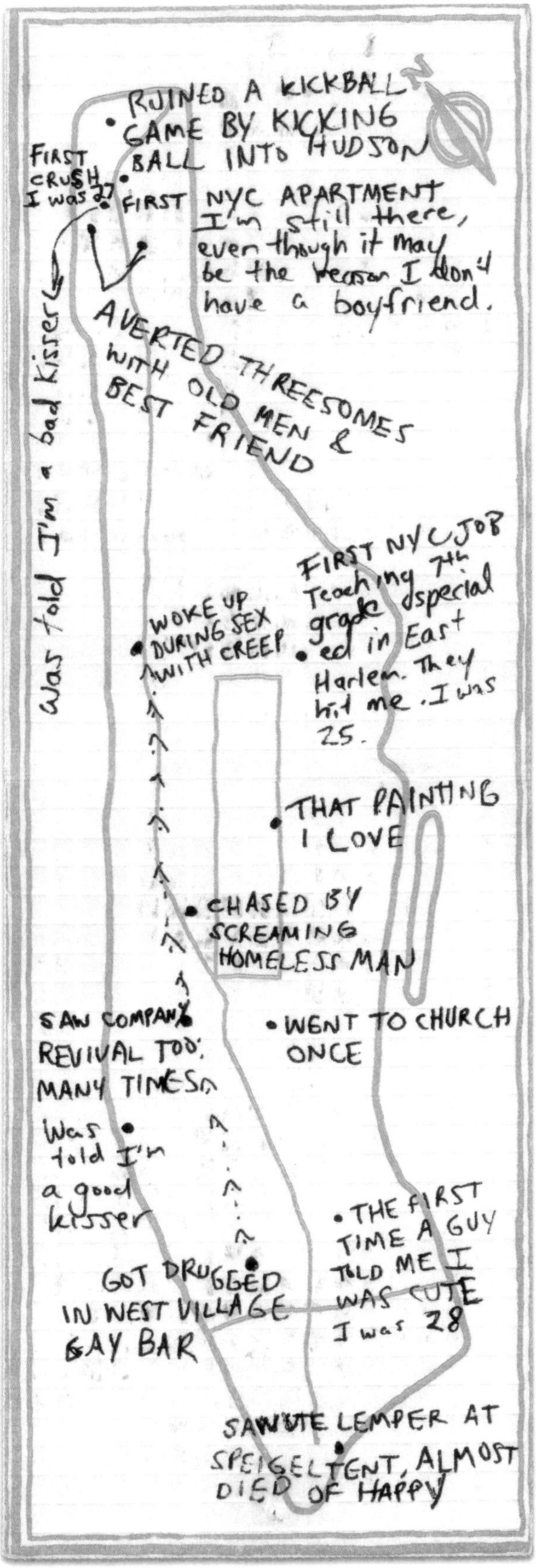

N

RUINED A KICKBALL GAME BY KICKING BALL INTO HUDSON

FIRST CRUSH I was 27

FIRST NYC APARTMENT I'm still there, even though it may be the reason I don't have a boyfriend.

Was told I'm a bad kisser

AVERTED THREESOMES WITH OLD MEN & BEST FRIEND

FIRST NYC JOB Teaching 7th grade special ed in East Harlem. They hit me. I was 25.

WOKE UP DURING SEX WITH CREEP

THAT PAINTING I LOVE

CHASED BY SCREAMING HOMELESS MAN

SAW COMPANY REVIVAL TOO MANY TIMES

WENT TO CHURCH ONCE

Was told I'm a good kisser

THE FIRST TIME A GUY TOLD ME I WAS CUTE I was 28

GOT DRUGGED IN WEST VILLAGE GAY BAR

SAW UTE LEMPER AT SPEIGELTENT, ALMOST DIED OF HAPPY

MAPS ARE MORE ABOUT THEIR MAKERS THAN THE PLACES THEY DESCRIBE.
MAP WHO YOU ARE. MAP WHERE YOU ARE. MAP THE FIRST SNOWFALL OR YOUR
FAVORITE CUP OF COFFEE. MAP THE INVISIBLE. MAP THE OBVIOUS.
MAP YOUR MEMORIES.
SUBMISSIONS ARE DUE AUGUST 15th, 2009. YOUR MANHATTAN MAY BE PUBLISHED
mapyourmemories.tumblr.com
USA FIRST-CLASS FOREVER
MAP YOUR MEMORIES
P.O. BOX 356196
BRIARWOOD, NY 11435
Copyright Rebecca Cooper 2009
YOU FOUND ME
SITTING ON THE STEPS (south side of East Houston)
Between Suffolk & Norfolk

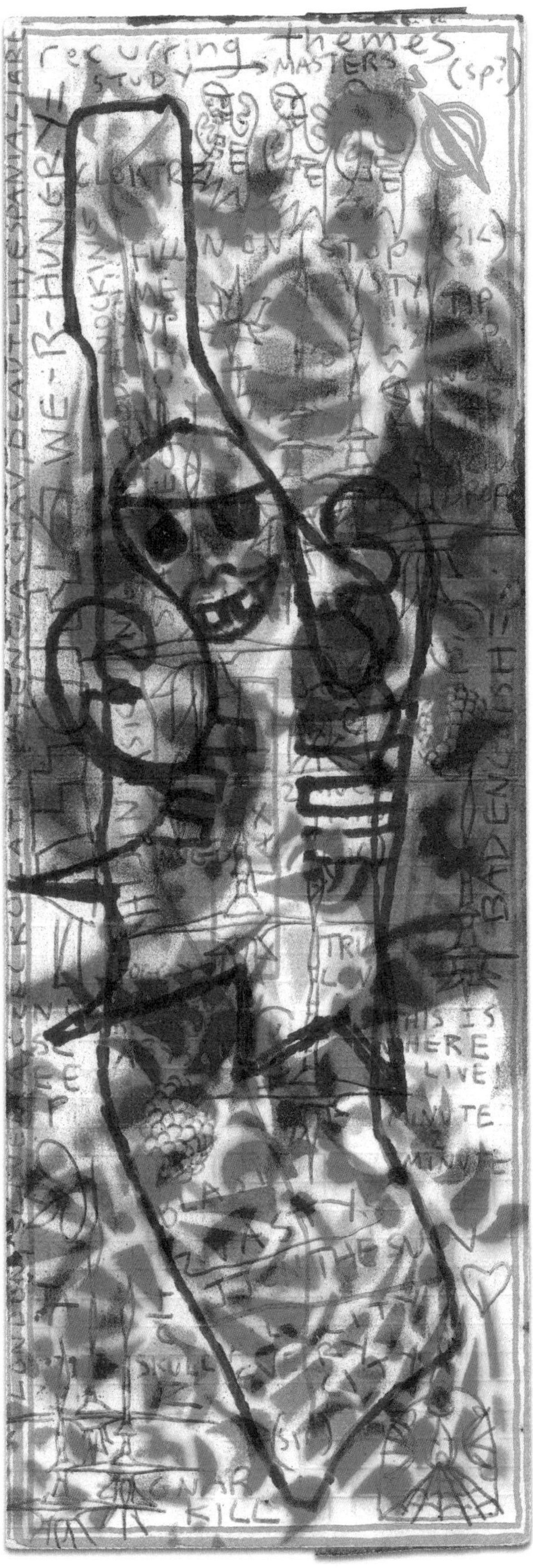
recurring themes (sp?)
STUDY
MASTERS
WE-R-HUNGRY
BAD ENGLISH
THIS IS HERE LIVE
SKULL
GNAR KILL

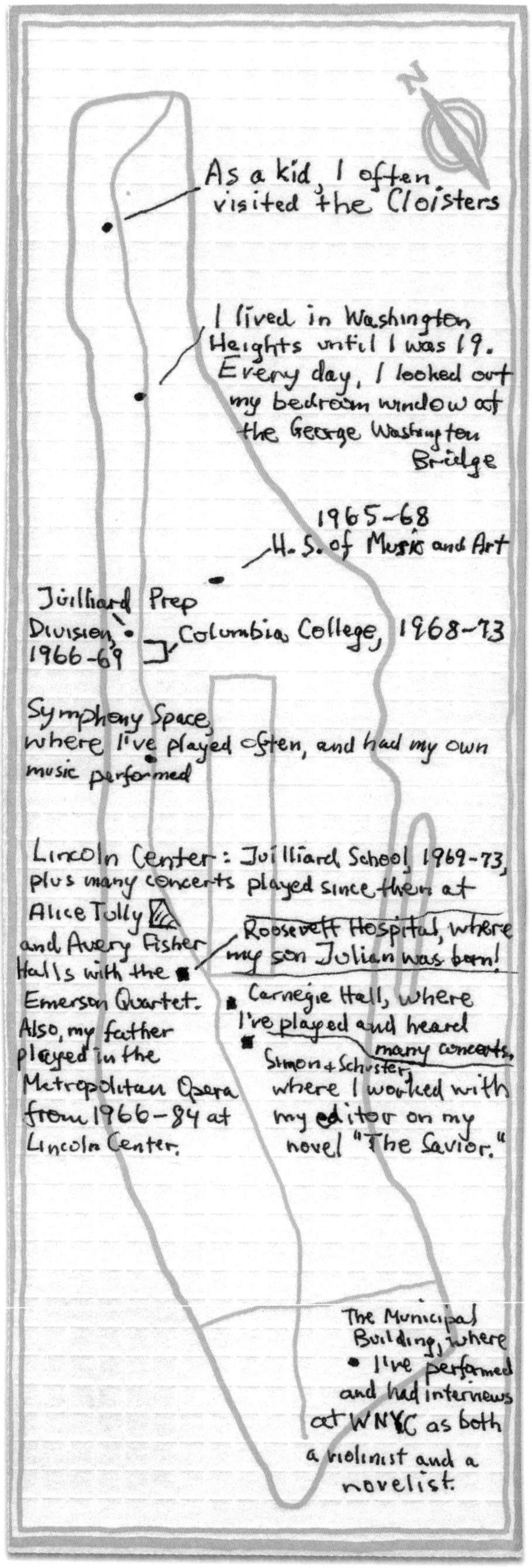

N

As a kid, I often visited the Cloisters

I lived in Washington Heights until I was 19. Every day, I looked out my bedroom window at the George Washington Bridge

1965–68 H. S. of Music and Art

Juilliard Prep Division 1966–69

Columbia College, 1968–73

Symphony Space, where I've played often, and had my own music performed

Lincoln Center: Juilliard School, 1969–73, plus many concerts played since then at Alice Tully and Avery Fisher Halls with the Emerson Quartet. Also, my father played in the Metropolitan Opera from 1966–84 at Lincoln Center.

Roosevelt Hospital, where my son Julian was born!

Carnegie Hall, where I've played and heard many concerts.

Simon & Schuster, where I worked with my editor on my novel "The Savior."

The Municipal Building, where I've performed and had interviews at WNYC as both a violinist and a novelist.

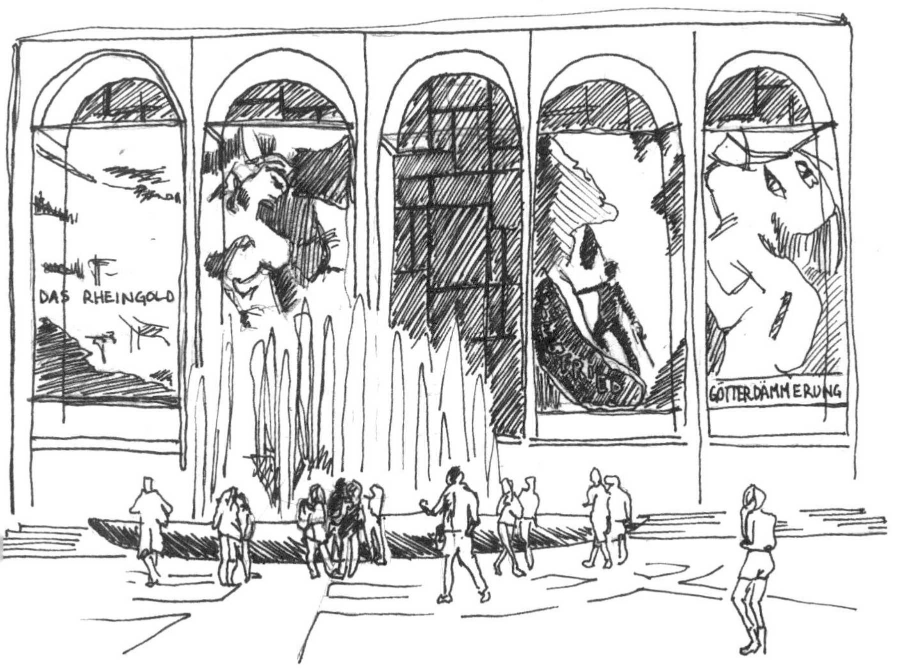

66TH STREET—LINCOLN CENTER, **3:31 P.M.**

Tables of used books. Piles of *Playbills*. Mysterious stacks of signed Philip Roth novels. Kirk Davidson, the bookseller, reclines as best he can on his folding chair. He used to reign over his stand on an upholstered seat—the tattered cloth was a landmark on the Upper West Side—but it's been ousted for the same reason that the last residents of Carnegie Hall were given the boot: The city's outgrown it. ■ A man digging through the trash for recycling nearby asks, "Can I have two maps? So I can keep one?" ■ At the onslaught of the 72nd Street crosswalk, Ama and I leave behind the crowd wearing black leggings and pushing running strollers and follow instead the cellos worn as backpacks. Snaking down Broadway, past the beds of white tulips, past the renovated Alice Tully Hall (where I can't help but remember a stranger's impromptu "These Foolish Things" that once rang out on the public piano parked there for an art installation), we walk until the Upper West Side opens to the white limestone expanse of Lincoln Center. The Met is preparing for its Ring Cycle, and a larger-than-life Siegfried banner announces the entrance of the opera house. ■ At 65th Street—Leonard Bernstein Place—Ama and I cheat off Broadway for a second and approach a young couple sitting on the granite edge of the Lincoln Center fountain. They have their Moleskines out and are labeling their sketches in German. I point to the map. They nod. "Anything," I say. They nod. I hand them each a map, and they slip the cards into the back pockets of their notebooks.

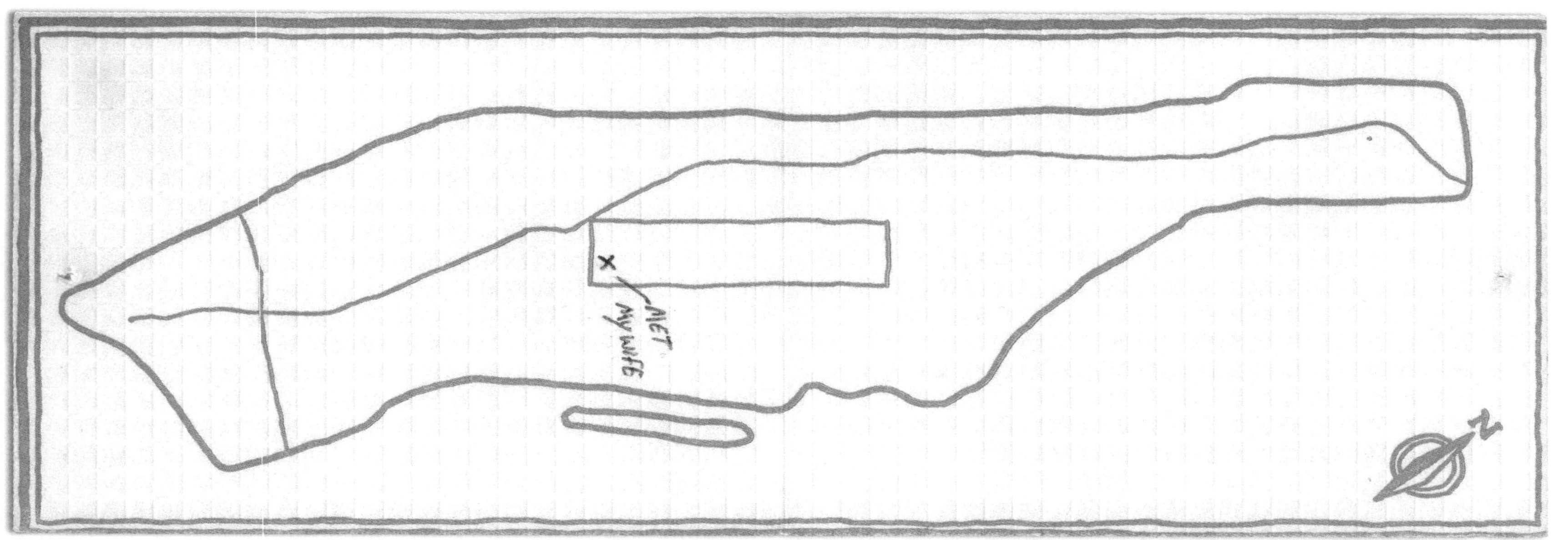
N
MET
My WIFE

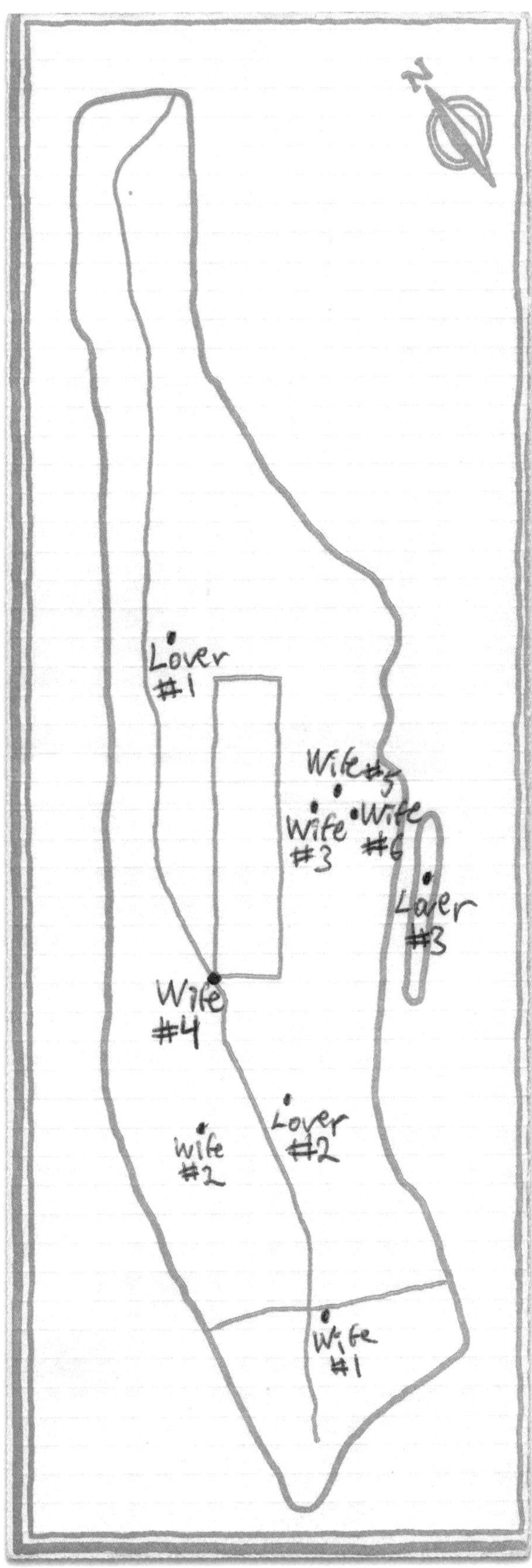
N
Lover
#1
Wife #5
Wife
#3
Wife
#6
Lover
#3
Wife
#4
Lover
#2
Wife
#2
Wife
#1

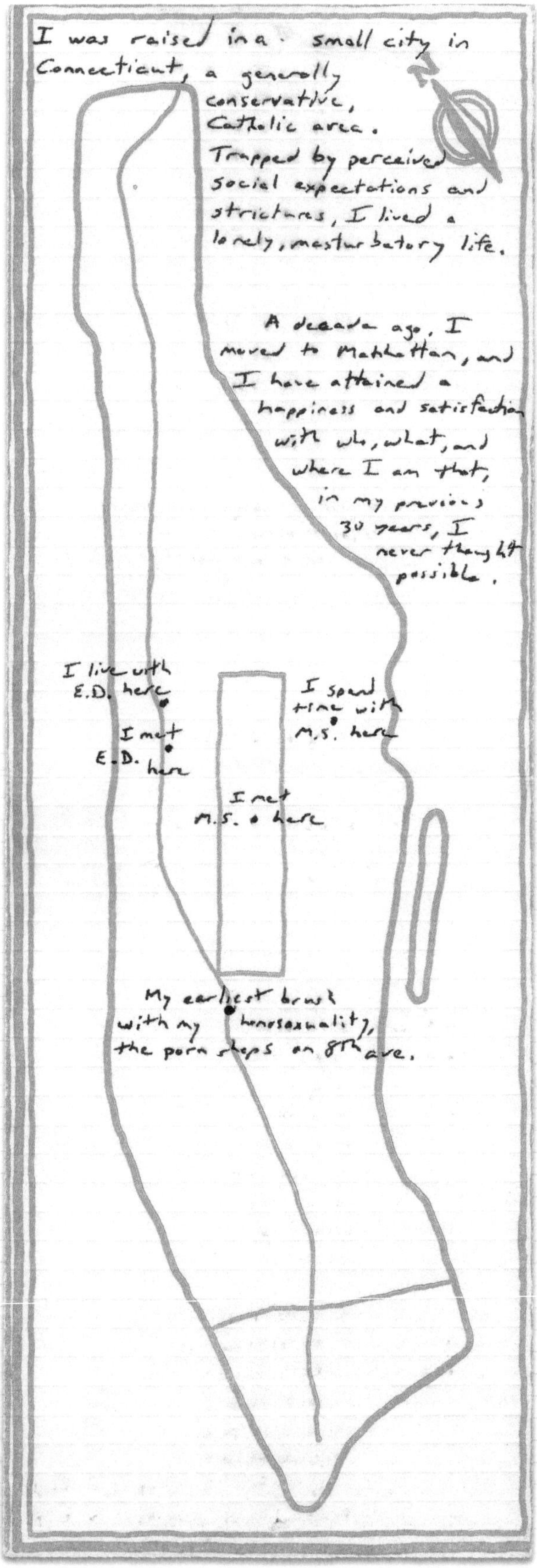

I was raised in a small city in Connecticut, a generally conservative, Catholic area. Trapped by perceived social expectations and strictures, I lived a lonely, masturbatory life.

A decade ago, I moved to Manhattan, and I have attained a happiness and satisfaction with who, what, and where I am that, in my previous 30 years, I never thought possible.

I live with E.D. here

I met E.D. here

I spend time with M.S. here

I met M.S. here

My earliest brush with my homosexuality, the porn shops on 8th ave.

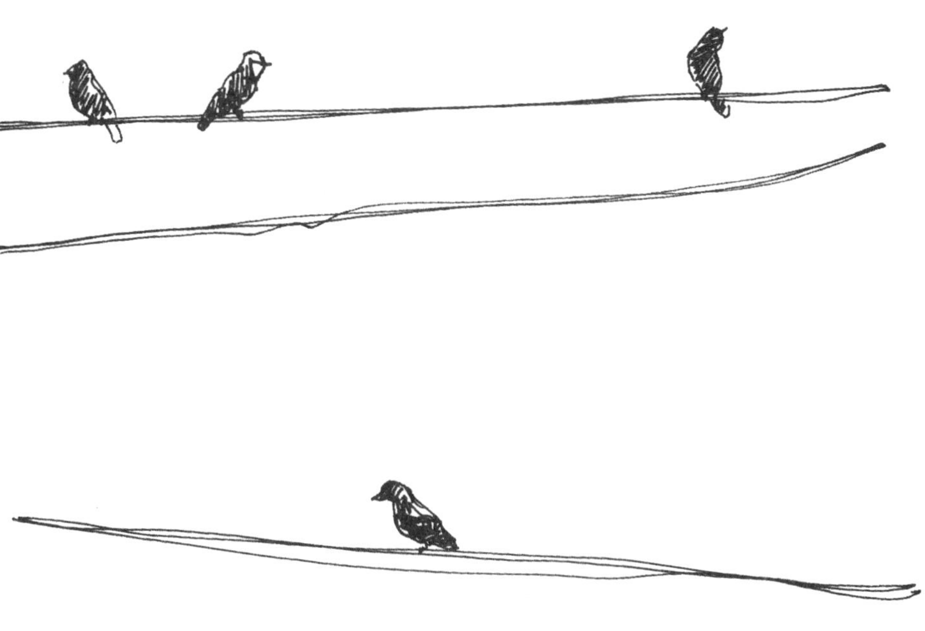

I was raised in a small city in Connecticut, a generally conservative, Catholic area. Trapped by perceived social expectations and strictures, I lived a lonely, masturbatory life.

A decade ago, I moved to Manhattan, and I have attained a happiness and satisfaction with who, what, and where I am that, in my previous 30 years, I never thought possible.

I live with E.D. here
I met E.D. here
I spend time with M.S. here
I met M.S. here

My earliest brush with my homosexuality, the porn shops on 8th ave.

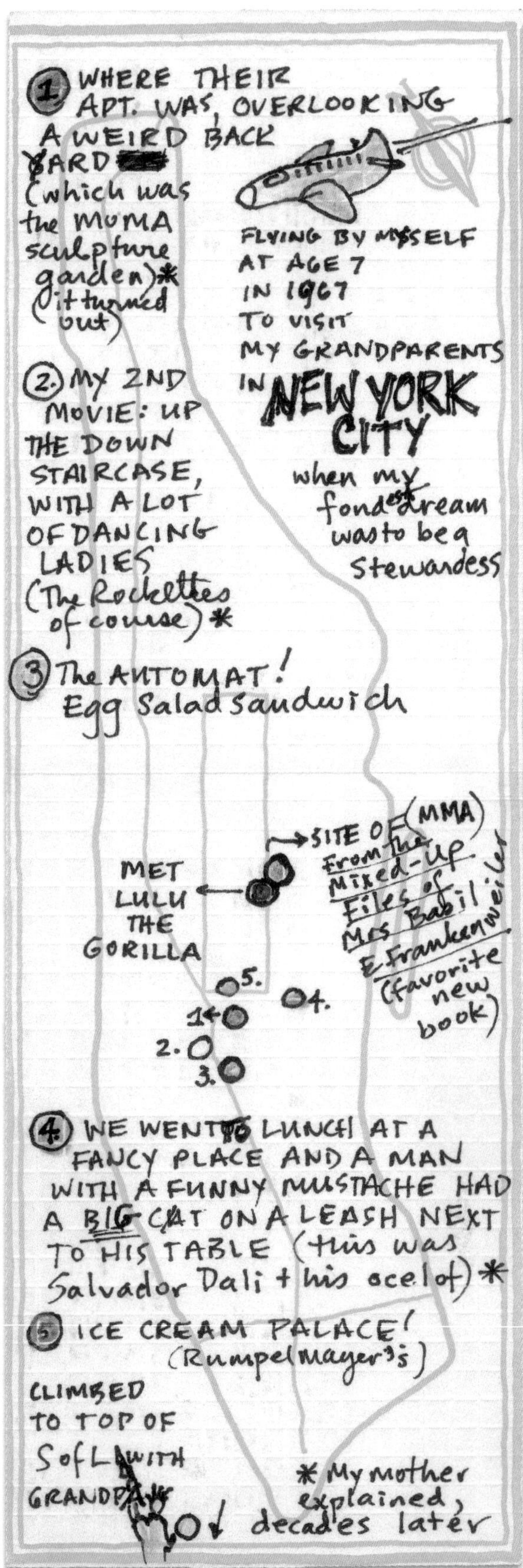
1 WHERE THEIR APT. WAS, OVERLOOKING A WEIRD BACK YARD (which was the MOMA sculpture garden)* (it turned out)
FLYING BY MYSELF AT AGE 7 IN 1967 TO VISIT MY GRANDPARENTS IN NEW YORK CITY when my fondest dream was to be a Stewardess
2. MY 2ND MOVIE: UP THE DOWN STAIRCASE, WITH A LOT OF DANCING LADIES (The Rockettes of course)*
3 The AUTOMAT! Egg Salad sandwich
SITE OF (MMA) From the Mixed-Up Files of Mrs Basil E. Frankenweiler (favorite new book)
MET LULU THE GORILLA
5.
4.
1.
2.
3.
4 WE WENT TO LUNCH AT A FANCY PLACE AND A MAN WITH A FUNNY MUSTACHE HAD A BIG CAT ON A LEASH NEXT TO HIS TABLE (this was Salvador Dali + his ocelot)*
5 ICE CREAM PALACE! (Rumpelmayer's)
CLIMBED TO TOP OF S of L WITH GRANDPA
* My mother explained, decades later

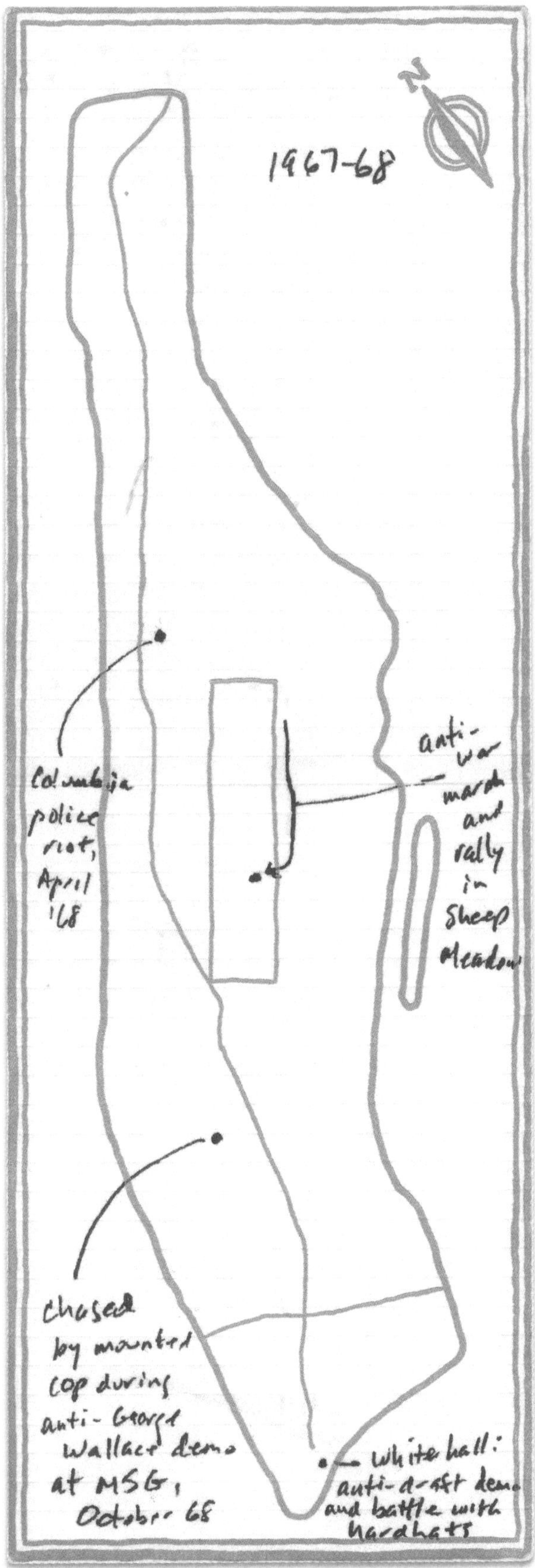
N
1967-68
Columbia police riot, April '68
anti-war march and rally in Sheep Meadow
chased by mounted cop during anti-George Wallace demo at MSG, October 68
White hall: anti-draft demo and battle with hardhats

59TH STREET—COLUMBUS CIRCLE, 3:50 P.M.

From the center of the rotary—Ama and I can see the horse-drawn carriages that line 59th Street and the trails in Central Park originally cut for them. Just inside, runners loop toward the dirt road of the Bridle Path. The park is emerald this time of year. ■ Like Broadway, Central Park was not part of the original plan that recast Manhattan as a grid. When a giant city park was first proposed in the 1850s, officials suggested Jones's Wood on the East side, between Third Avenue and the East River and 66th and 75th streets. It was only at the last minute that today's more central location was suggested. ■ The park's designers, Calvert Vaux and Frederick Law Olmsted, created a masterpiece of illusion. They worked with the landscape—the Manhattan schist outcroppings and the boulders deposited eons ago by the Wisconsin Ice Sheet—but took substantial pains to elevate its beauty. What seems natural today is almost completely manmade. The lakes are all artificial; nearly every foot of soil was raised or lowered. ■ Ama and I stroll into the park. Even just a few feet within its boundaries, the park feels full of magic. The paths pull us forward. One leads to the carousel that once cost ten cents and was turned by a blind mule and a horse that lived in its basement. Another leads to SummerStage, the outdoor venue built where an exquisite casino used to stand. Our path leads to a couple sitting in the shade of an old oak. I give them two maps, but the woman hesitates. She glances at the man next to her and hands hers back to me. ■ "We met here forty years ago," she explains. "We lived on the other side of the park, but moved away when our daughter went to college." The wife looks at her husband's map and points to the white space to the right of the park. "We're about to see our first grandkid." ■ "Can we fill it out together?" he asks, smiling. ■ "Of course," I say. ■ Ama and I turn to head out of the park. I know we're about to walk onto Broadway again—the part that faces the glittering Time Warner Center just south of Trump Towers—but for now all I can see are the trees that drape the benches, and I'm happy to have the city disappear for a second longer.

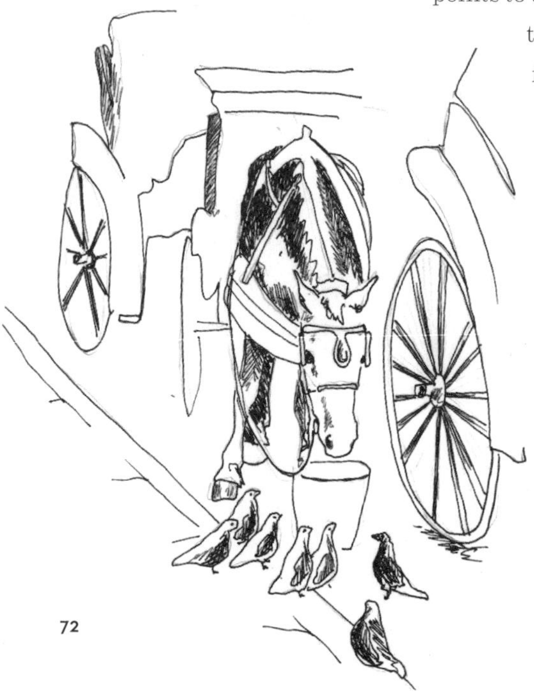

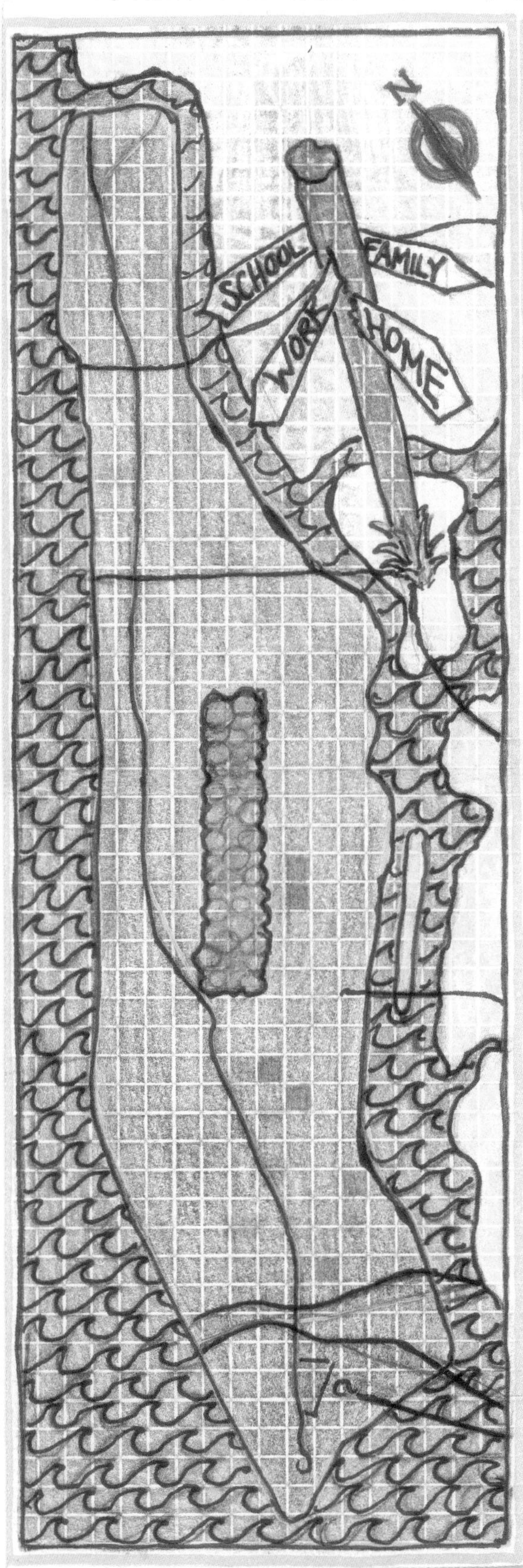
N
SCHOOL
FAMILY
WORK
HOME

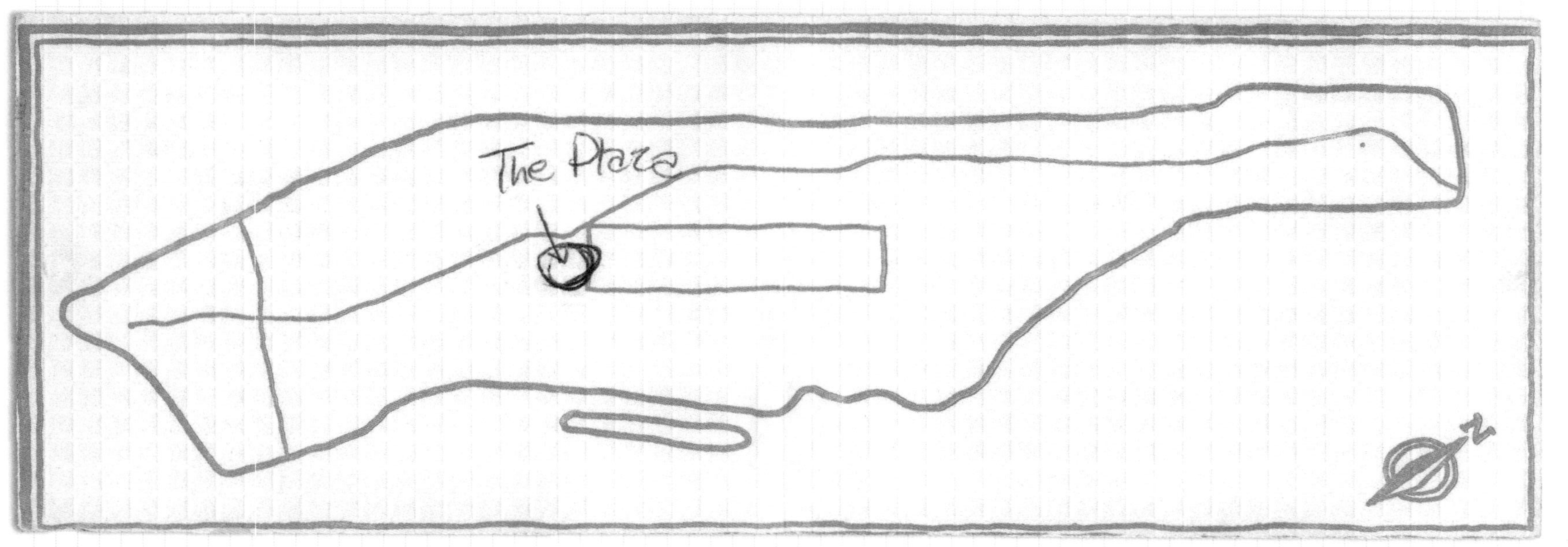
The Plaza
N

I was probably about the same age as the young woman who approached me [with a blank map of Manhattan] when I first arrived in NYC, although my heart had arrived years before that– the Christmas of 1958, to be precise, when I was 7 years old and I received a copy of Eloise *who took me through those "revolving doors with a P on them" for the first time. It was a circuitous route between the ages 7 and 22 getting to Manhattan but one that I now realize was as magical as inevitable. ■ I'd like to say my initial introduction to life in Manhattan was magical but it was the 70's, a particularly dark time in NYC history, not to mention my husband and I were dirt poor so magic was in short supply. Central Park simply wasn't an option back then even though we were often obliged to take our lives in our hands and walk the width of it from our grim apartment directly over a dry cleaners on East 70th to Columbus Circle where we worked. Suffice it to say tea at the Palm Court or dinners in The Oak Room weren't options. ■ Manhattan when you're poor isn't a whole lot of fun. But being young and too dumb and naïve to realize that having limited options wasn't actually all that romantic, we not only made the best of our early years, we made our own magic that has held us close for 37 years. And then there was the magic of our daughter who still lives in Manhattan, only a few blocks from Central Park, and has her own memories of numerous teas at the Palm Court with me and Eloise and even the occasional stuffy family event at The Oak Room. ■ I haven't been back to The Plaza since it finally re-opened even though I hear that The Oak Room is open to the public. I'm not sure why I haven't gone in yet because I have no doubt the magic, along with Eloise's portrait, is still there somewhere despite all the tarting-up and exclusivity that comes with a 5-mil-and-up-per-unit price tag. Perhaps I'm just waiting for the right moment–or an invitation. In the meantime, I'll continue to look forward to the next time I walk through "the revolving doors with a P on them" and see what Eloise is up to these days. ■ Oooooh, I absolutely love New York! I absolutely do.*

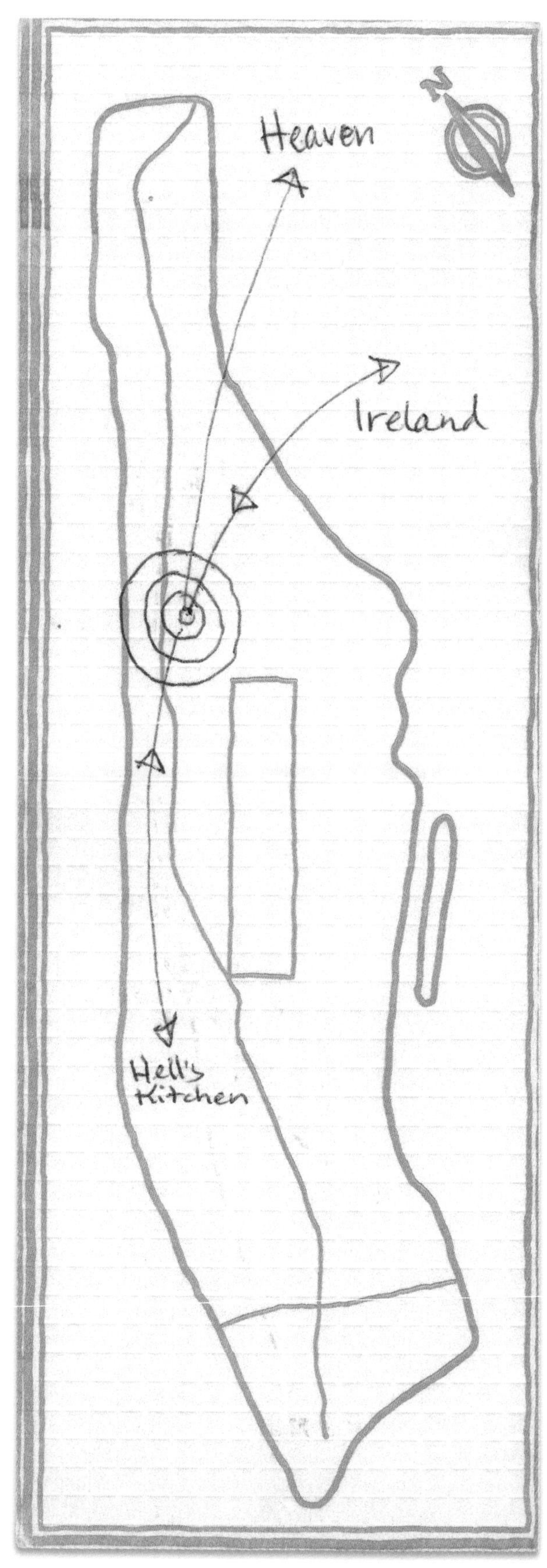
N
Heaven
Ireland
Hell's
Kitchen

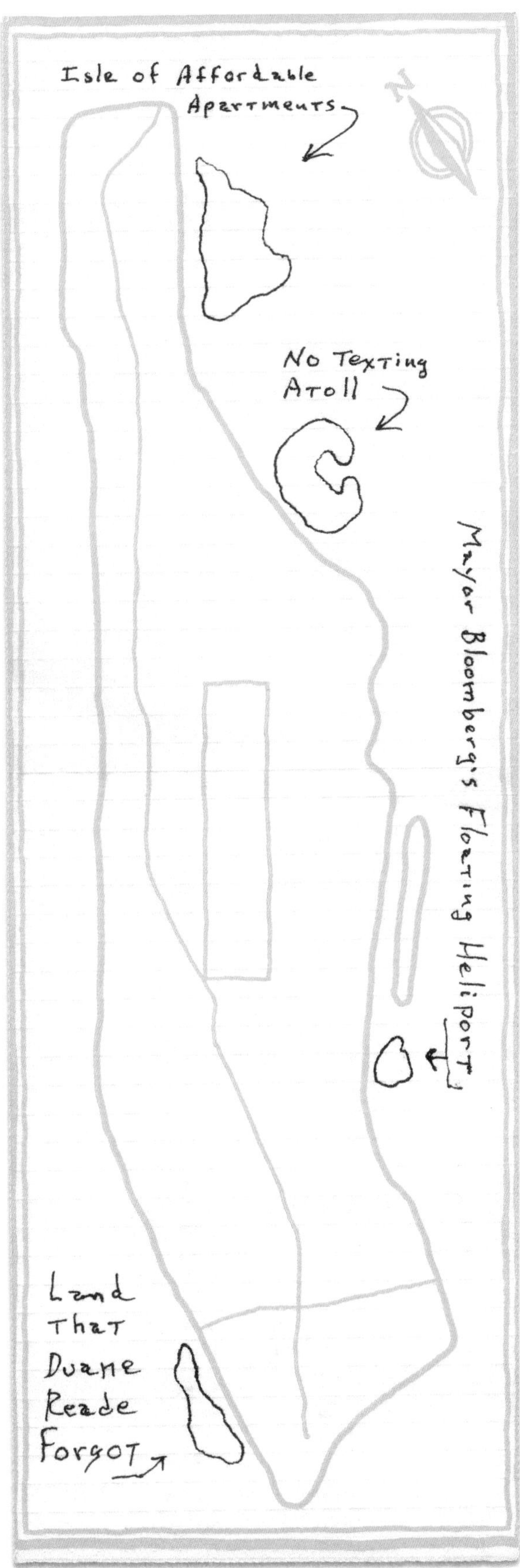
Isle of Affordable Apartments
No Texting Atoll
Mayor Bloomberg's Floating Heliport
Land That Duane Reade Forgot

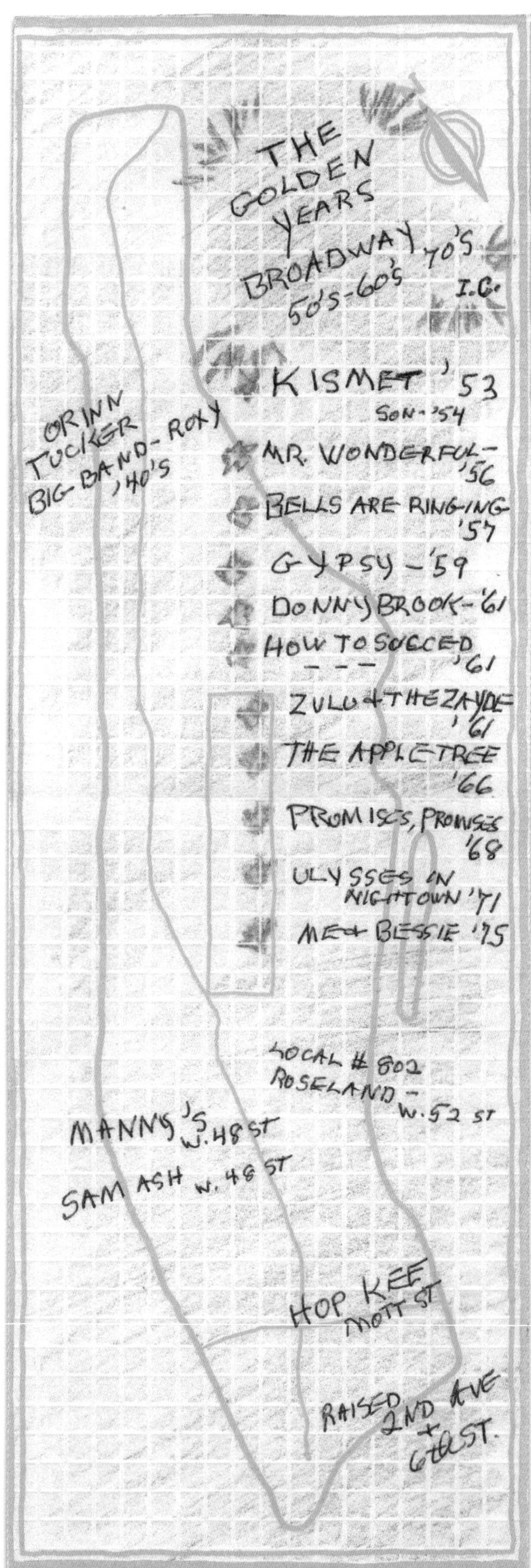
THE GOLDEN YEARS
BROADWAY 50'S-60'S 70'S
I.C.
KISMET '53
SON-'54
MR. WONDERFUL-'56
BELLS ARE RINGING '57
GYPSY-'59
DONNYBROOK-'61
HOW TO SUCCEED --- '61
ZULU + THE ZAYDE '61
THE APPLE TREE '66
PROMISES, PROMISES '68
ULYSSES IN NIGHTOWN '71
ME + BESSIE '75
ORINN TUCKER BIG BAND-ROXY '40'S
LOCAL # 802 ROSELAND-W. 52 ST
MANNY'S W. 48 ST
SAM ASH W. 48 ST
HOP KEE MOTT ST
RAISED 2ND AVE + 6TH ST.

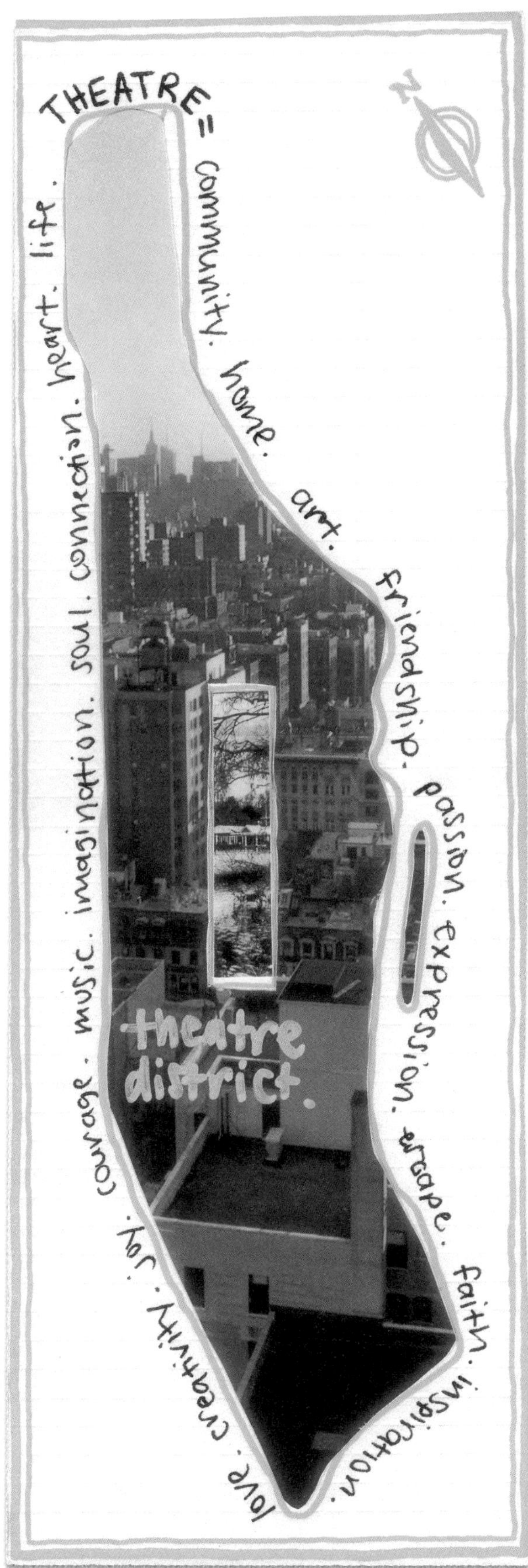
THEATRE= community. home. art. friendship. passion. expression. escape. faith. inspiration. love. creativity. joy. courage. music. imagination. soul. connection. heart. life.
theatre district.

42ND STREET—TIMES SQUARE, 4:20 P.M.

It's true. Manhattan is a story of movement. People talk fast and walk fast; the subway service never (well, almost never) stops; scaffolding goes up, comes down; people move from Bed-Stuy and Bushwick to Fort Greene and Greenpoint to the East and West Villages to the Upper East and West Sides. But Times Square is where that movement comes to a halt. The only things that zoom here are the billboards and the fast-talking *"Extratickets!LionKingtonight"* scalpers. To better take in the sights, tourists move with the ease of molasses, and many give up to lounge on the mid-Broadway plazas. They pose for photos with the policemen on horseback who, on this gorgeous spring afternoon, could almost pass for decoration. The theaters are still here, frozen on their march up Broadway by the introduction of movies, but long gone are the Tenderloin District days. In the 1970s, the precincts in Times Square consistently placed first and second in the city in total number of felonies. Today, the sinister side of Times Square seems to have been swept away with the New Year's confetti. The Naked Cowboy with his strategically placed guitar is about as much flesh as today's Times Square sees. Ama and I try to hand maps to a variety of people, but aside from tourists and a Gray Line bus tour manager, the only people we convince are a street cart vendor and a Japanese portrait sketcher whose charcoaled thumbs smudge the map as he tucks it into his pocket. Two hundred more maps to go, and 4 more miles.

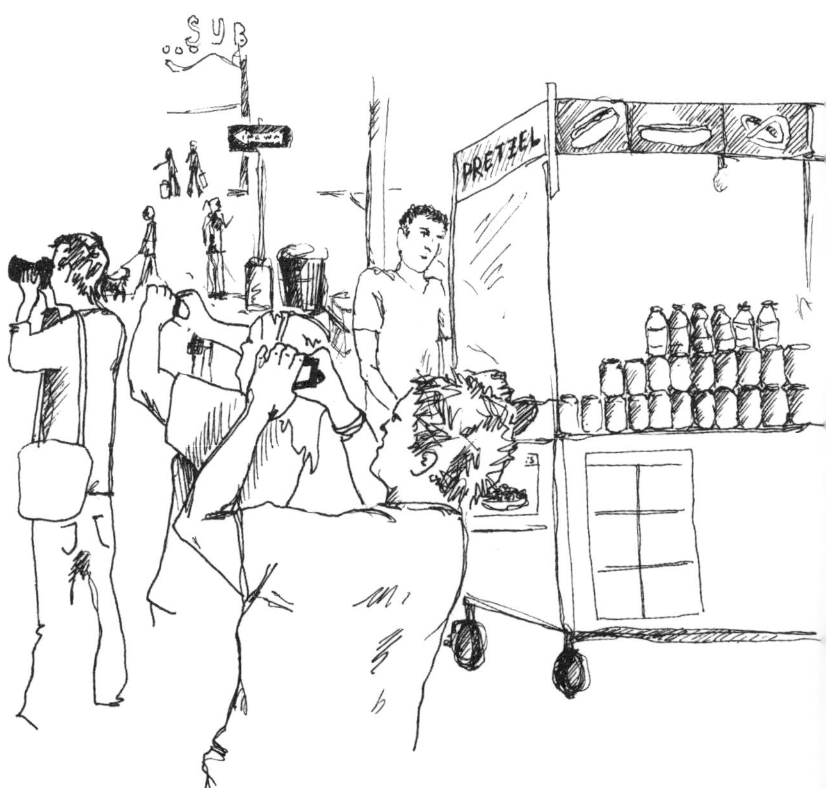

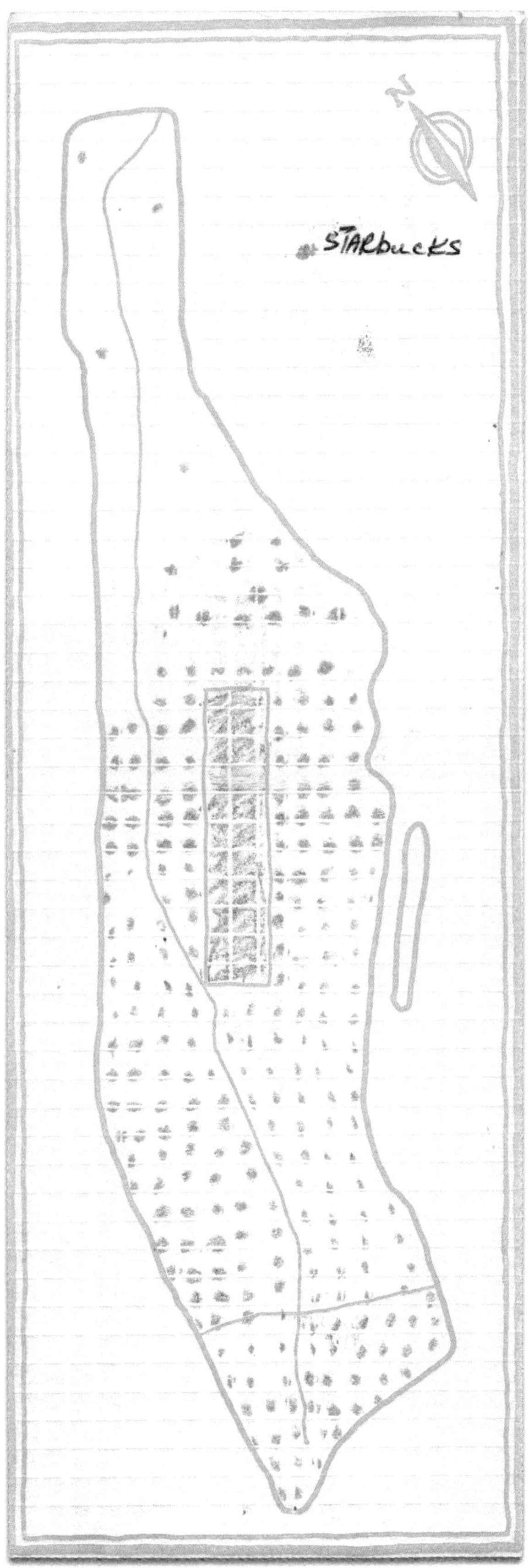
N
STARbucks

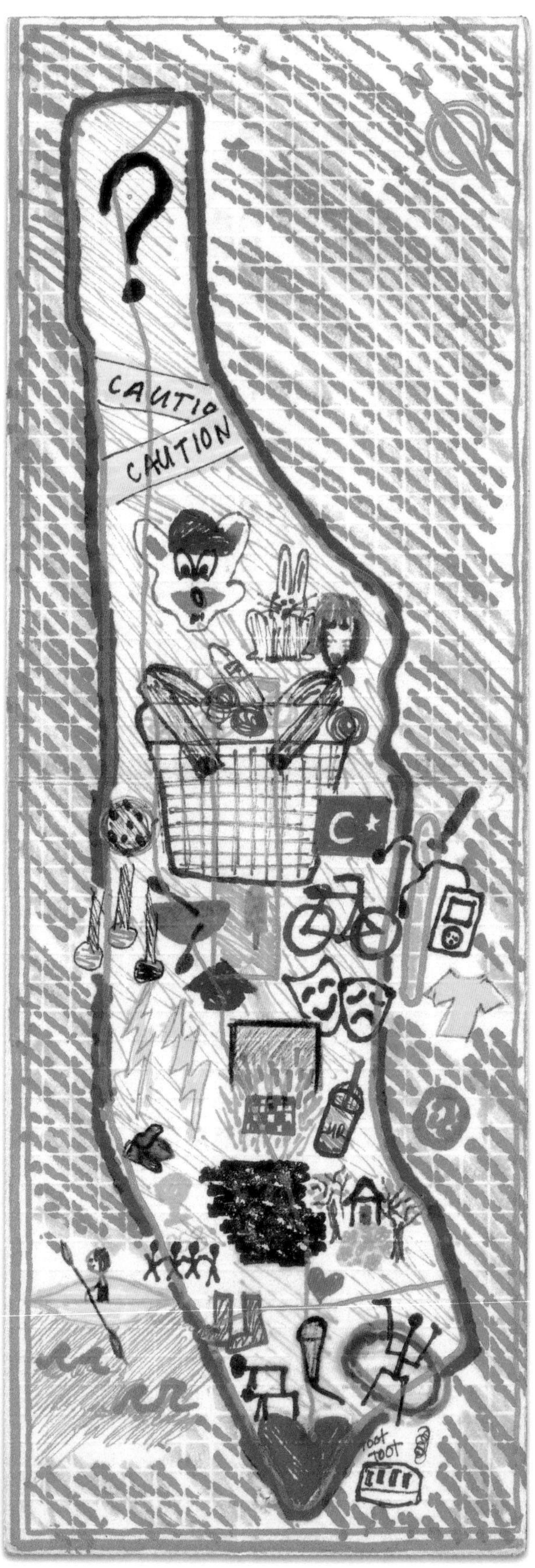
CAUTIO
CAUTION
TOOT
TOOT

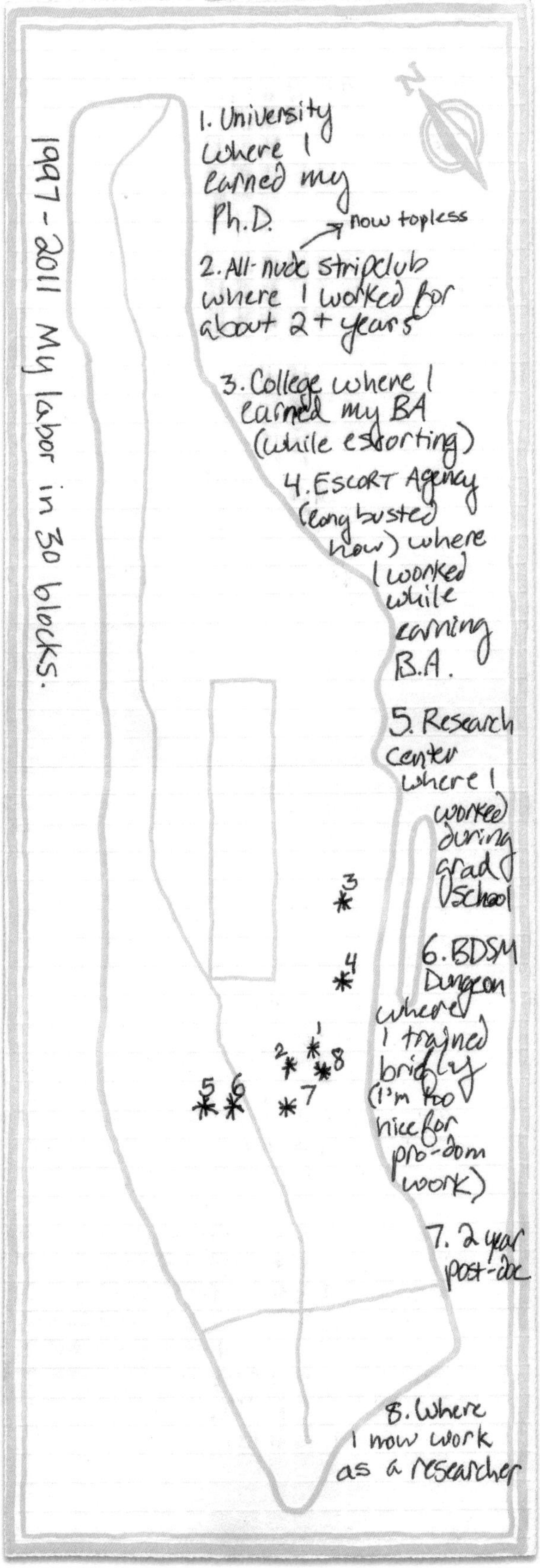

1997-2011 My labor in 30 blocks.

N

1. University where I earned my Ph.D.

→ now topless

2. All-nude stripclub where I worked for about 2+ years

3. College where I earned my BA (while escorting)

4. ESCORT Agency (long busted now) where I worked while earning B.A.

5. Research center where I worked during grad school

6. BDSM Dungeon where I trained briefly (I'm too nice for pro-dom work)

7. 2 year post-doc

8. Where I now work as a researcher

3 *

4 *

1 *

2 *

8 *

5 *

6 *

7 *

A: my childhood home
B: my first school (elementary)
C: my second school (elementary)
D: third school (middle)
E: high school; my first kiss
F: my first best friend's house
G: my second best friend's house
H: first make-out
I: my second girlfriend's house
J: my first break-up
K: waiting in line overnight at Sh. in the Pk.
L: first time my wife-to-be had dinner with my parents.
M: my pediatrician
N: where I went bowling with my HS girlfriend
O: closest family friend's home
P: my first home with my wife
Q: where my parents met

R: where my first g.friend & I got together (it was a bagel place)
S: my favorite playground as a child
T: my favorite coffee shop today
U: my three friends from school C— sad years
V: favorite Indian restaurants – where we went when I graduated HS & grad school.

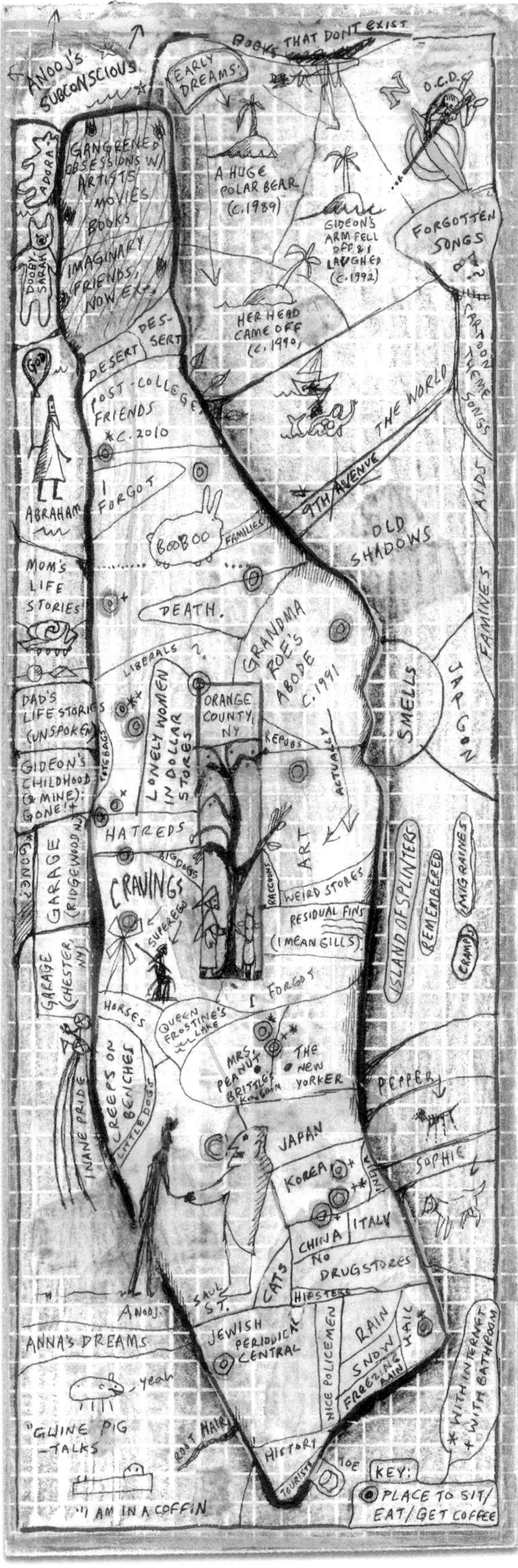
BOOKS THAT DON'T EXIST
ANOOJ'S SUBCONSCIOUS
EARLY DREAMS.
O.C.D.
N
ADORA
GANGRENED OBSESSIONS W/ ARTISTS, MOVIES, BOOKS
IMAGINARY FRIENDS, NOW EX.
A HUGE POLAR BEAR (C.1989)
GIDEON'S ARM FELL OFF & I LAUGHED (C.1992)
FORGOTTEN SONGS
DOOBY SARAH
HER HEAD CAME OFF (C.1990)
CARTOON THEME SONGS
DESERT
DESERT
GOD
POST-COLLEGE FRIENDS *C.2010
THE WORLD
I FORGOT
9TH AVENUE
AIDS
ABRAHAM
BOOBOO
FAMILIES
OLD SHADOWS
MOM'S LIFE STORIES!
DEATH.
FAMINES
GRANDMA ROE'S ABODE C.1991
LIBERALS
SMELLS
JARGON
DAD'S LIFE STORIES (UNSPOKEN)
LONELY WOMEN IN DOLLAR STORES
ORANGE COUNTY, NY
REPUBS
ACTUALLY
GIDEON'S CHILDHOOD (& MINE): GONE!
TOTE BAGS
HATREDS
ART
ISLAND OF SPLINTERS
REMEMBERED
MIGRAINES
GONE?
GARAGE (RIDGEWOOD NJ)
BIG DOGS
CRAVINGS
RACCOONS
WEIRD STORES
RESIDUAL FINS (I MEAN GILLS)
SUPEREGO
GARAGE (CHESTER, NY)
CRAMPS
I FORGOT
HORSES
QUEEN FROSTINE'S LAKE
MRS. PEANUT BRITTLE'S KINGDOM
THE NEW YORKER
CREEPS ON BENCHES
LITTLE DOGS
PEPPER
INANE PRIDE
JAPAN
KOREA
INDIA
SOPHIE
ITALY
CHINA
NO DRUGSTORES
CATS
SAUL ST.
HIPSTERS
ANOOJ.
JEWISH PERIODICAL CENTRAL
NICE POLICEMEN
RAIN
SNOW
HAIL
FREEZING RAIN
ANNA'S DREAMS
yeah
*WITH INTERNET
*WITH BATHROOM
"GUINE PIG" TALKS
ROOT HAIR
HISTORY
TOURISTS
TOE
KEY:
PLACE TO SIT/ EAT/ GET COFFEE
"I AM IN A COFFIN

LIANA FINCK

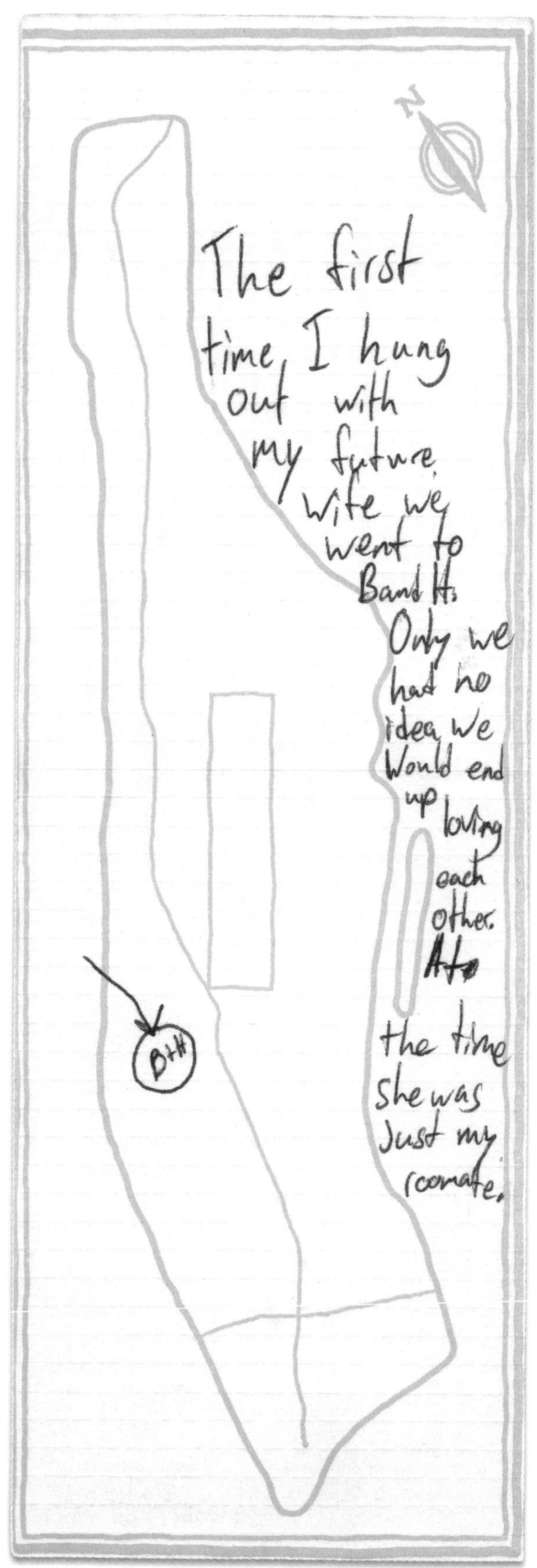
N
The first time, I hung out with my future wife we went to Band H. Only we had no idea we Would end up loving each other. At the time she was Just my roomate.
B+H

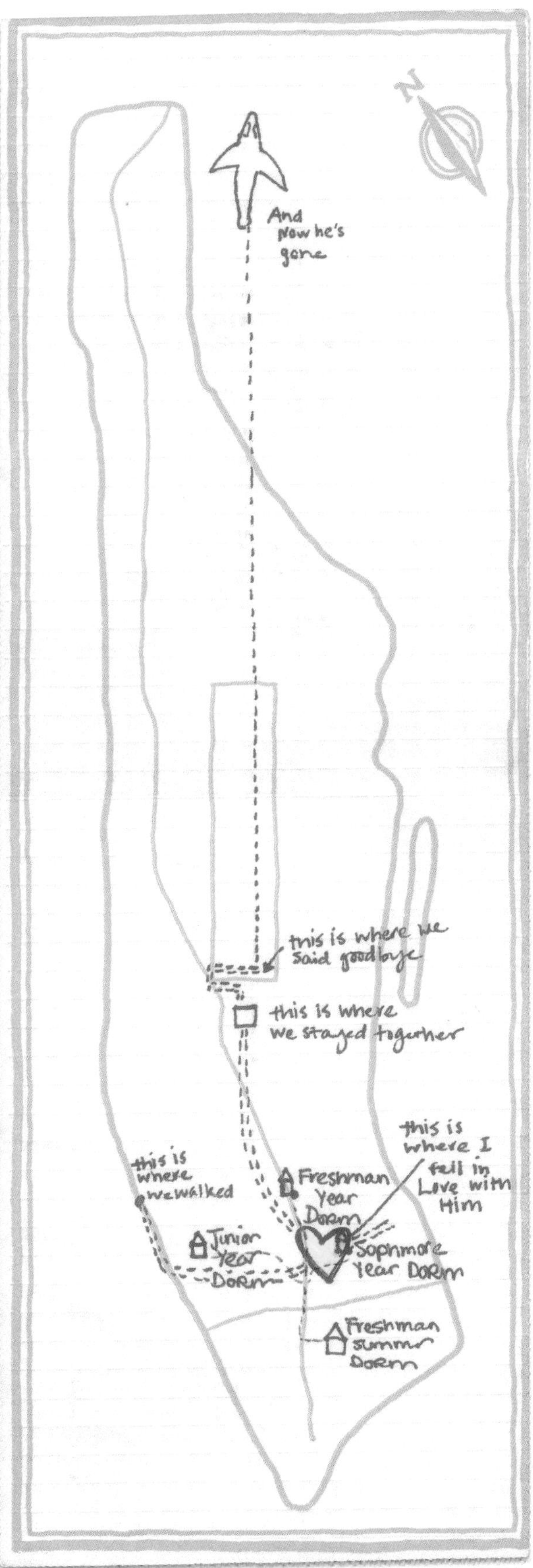
N
And
Now he's
gone
this is where we
said goodbye
this is where
we stayed together
this is
where I
fell in
Love with
Him
this is
where
we walked
Freshman
Year
Dorm
Junior
Year
Dorm
Sophmore
Year Dorm
Freshman
summer
Dorm

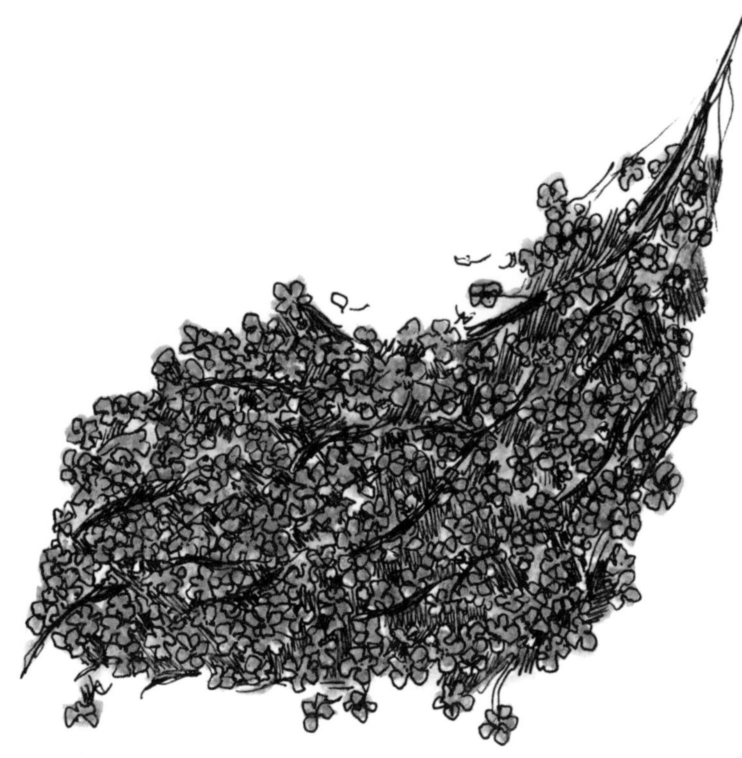

23RD STREET—CHERRY BLOSSOMS IN MADISON SQUARE PARK, 4:53 P.M.

Thirty-fourth Street speeds by. Or maybe we speed by it. ■ Ama and I cut through the no-man's-land (Lower Garment District? Flatiron? Upper Chelsea?) of Broadway between Herald Square and 24th Street until we reach the oasis of Madison Square Park. A street klezmer band greets visitors at the entrance. A photographer asks me to pose for a large-format picture in return for taking a map. "No, no—just tilt your head a bit to the right," he says. "Stay there." I freeze for what feels like three minutes. ■ A dog on a fur blanket snuggles his owner, also surrounded by furs too warm for this spring breeze. "What a curious idea!" the owner says. ■ A cyclist chases me through the park to ask for a map. ■ After the fourth old man in a row, Ama needs to remind me to stop handing maps to elderly gentlemen reading on benches. So instead, I run up to people on line at Shake Shack. ■ Outside the park, a deli owner who turns out to also be a professional cyclist asks if I wanna see his legs. He tells me the story of serial killers in Tompkins Square Park, about the forty miles he bikes every day to and from Hoboken, and about the importance of eating right, treating your body well. I decline the Pepsi he offers after his lecture.

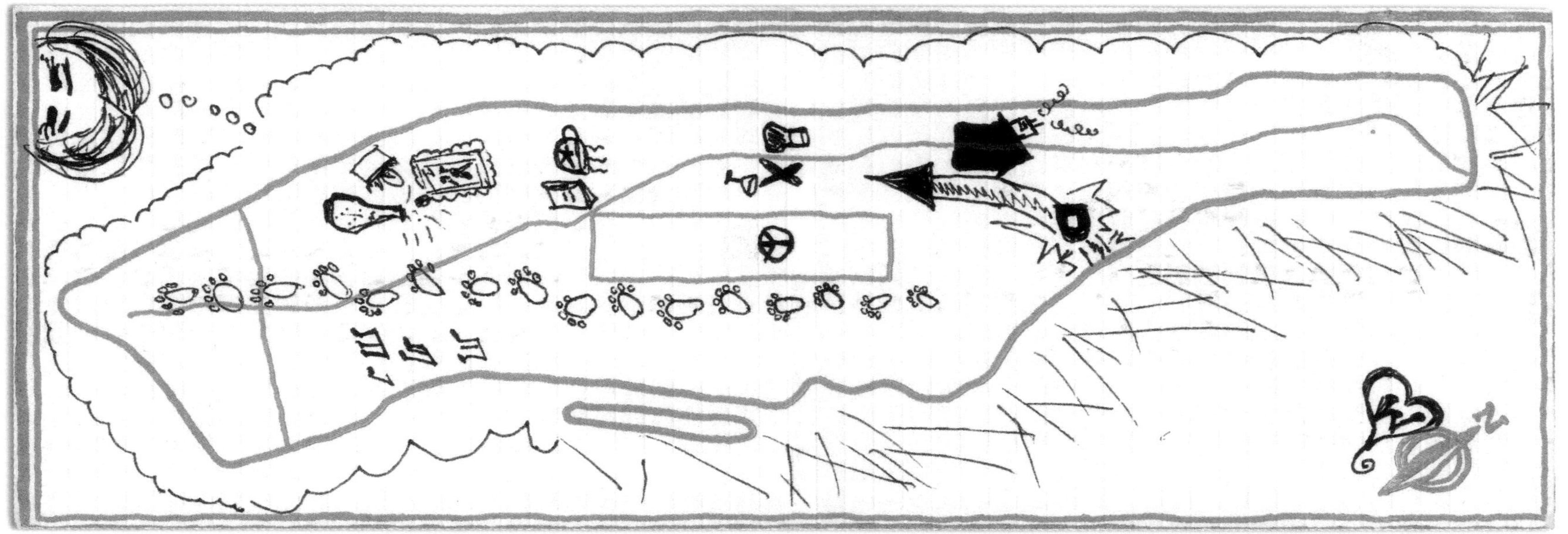

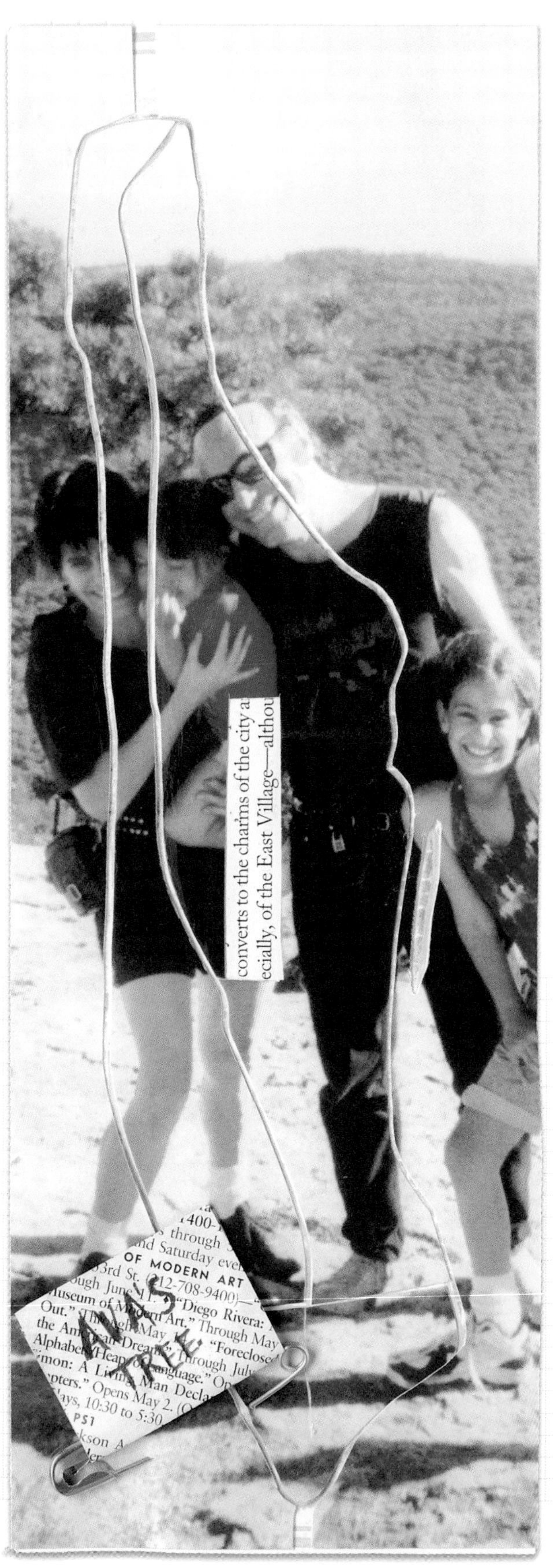
converts to the charms of the city a
ecially, of the East Village—althou
through
Saturday
OF MODERN ART
3rd St. (212-708-9400)—
"Diego Rivera:
Out."
Art." Through May
the
"Foreclosed
Alphabet
Through July
mon: A
Man Decla
Opens May 2.
10:30 to 5:30
PS1
AVA'S
TREE

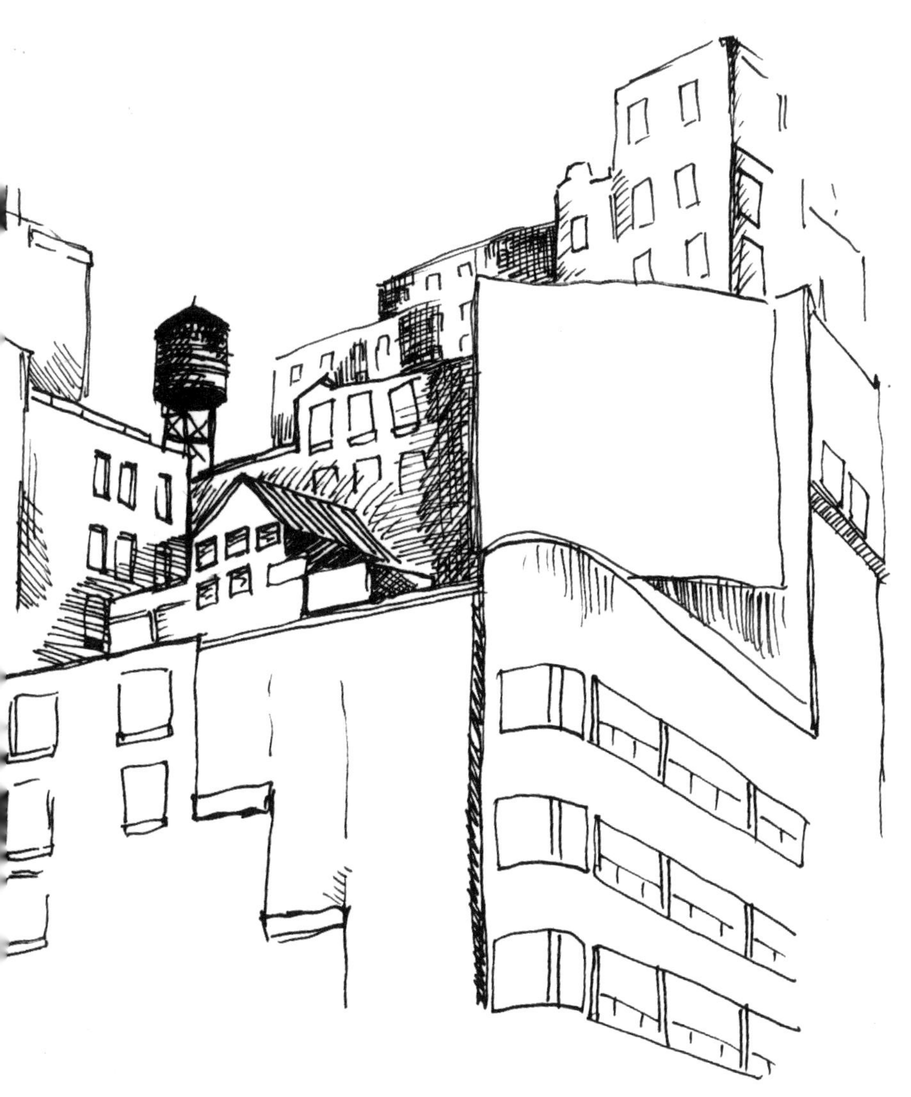

When I heard about [this project], I knew my map would have a photo . . . and initially I thought it would be of my sister, Ava. ■ When someone passes away, they are everywhere (at least I really believe that), and Ava is nowhere more than at every turn I make in the city. I struggled for a long (long!) time deciding how to realize my idea—photo on top? around? superimposed?—and then it hit me. The problem wasn't how to insert Ava into the map. The problem was that it wasn't just Ava who belonged there. My whole family is in my life in the city—the four of us as a unit—and the city courses through our veins, carrying us along its life like a river. ■ So here we are! The city is us, and we are the city. ■ P.S. Just in case you were wondering, Ava always wore safety pin earrings. Hence, the safety pin.

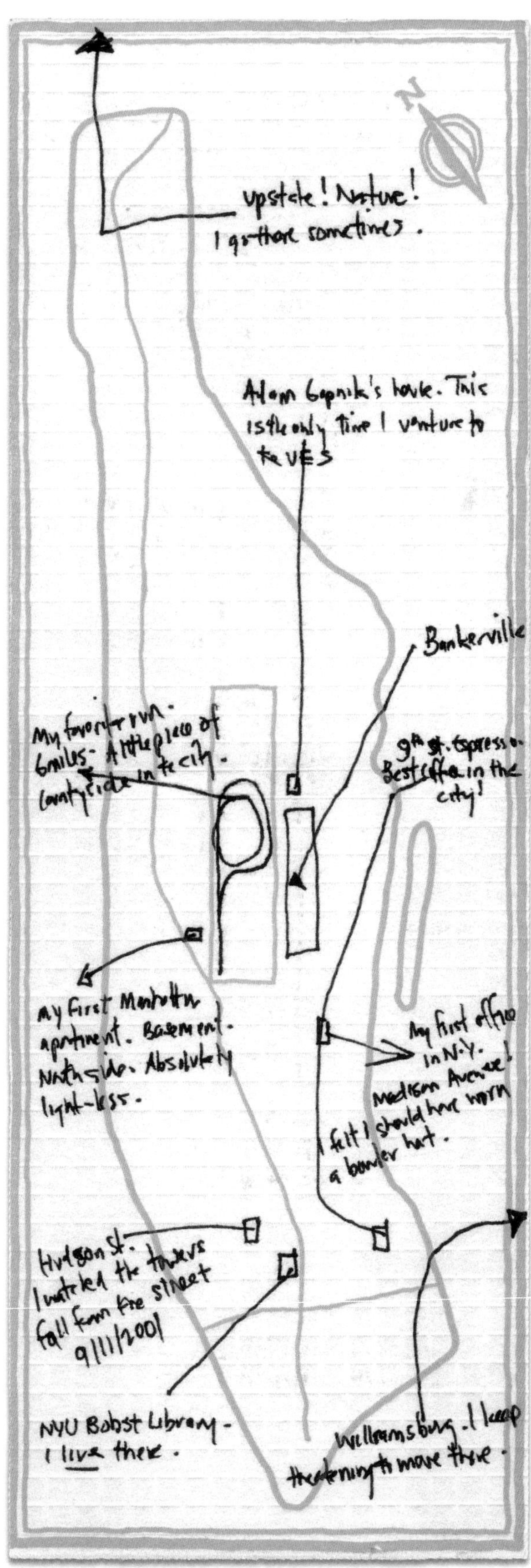
N
upstate! Nature!
I go there sometimes.
Adam Gopnik's house. This is the only time I venture to the UES
Bankerville
My favorite run. 6 miles. A little piece of countryside in the city.
9th St. Espresso. Best coffee in the city!
My first Manhattan apartment. Basement. North side. Absolutely light-less.
My first office in N.Y.
Madison Avenue!
I felt I should have worn a bowler hat.
Hudson St.
I watched the towers fall from the street
9/11/2001
NYU Bobst Library -
I live there.
Williamsburg. I keep threatening to move there.

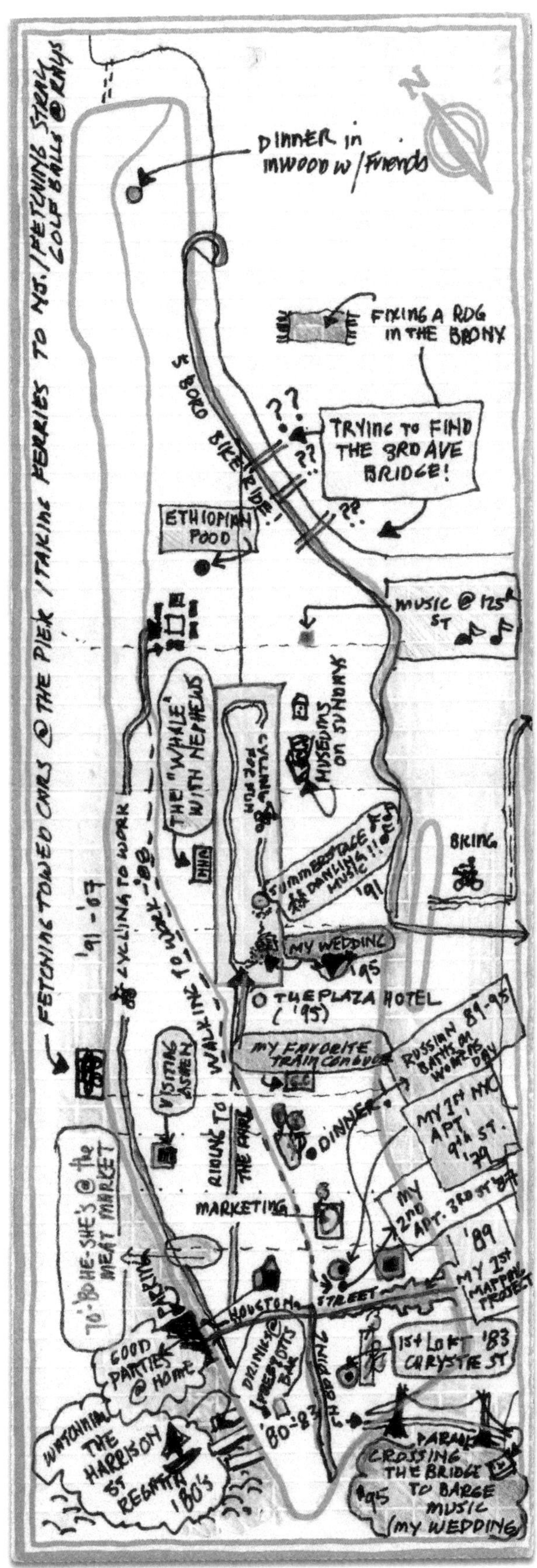

FETCHING TOWED CARS @ THE PIER / TAKING FERRIES TO NJ. / FETCHING STRAY GOLF BALLS
DINNER in INWOOD w/ friends
FIXING A RUG IN THE BRONX
TRYING TO FIND THE 3RD AVE BRIDGE!
BIKE RIDE
ETHIOPIAN FOOD
MUSIC @ 125th ST
THE "WHALE" WITH NEPHEWS
CYCLING FOR FUN
MUSEUMS ON SUNDAYS
BIKING
SUMMERSTAGE DANCING MUSIC '91
MY WEDDING '95
'91-'07 CYCLING TO WORK
WALKING TO WORK '88
THE PLAZA HOTEL ('95)
MY FAVORITE TRAIN CONDUCTOR
RUSSIAN BATHS ON WOMEN'S DAY 89-95
MY 1st NYC APT 9th ST. '79
DINNER
RIDING TO THE PARK
MARKETING
MY 2ND APT. 3RD ST '87
'89 MY 1st MAPPING PROJECT
'70-'80 HE-SHE'S @ the MEAT MARKET
PARKING
HOUSTON STREET
GOOD PARTIES @ HOME
'80-'83
1st LOFT '83 CHRYSTIE ST
WEDDING
WATCHING THE HARRISON ST REGATTA '80's
PARADE CROSSING THE BRIDGE TO BARGE MUSIC (MY WEDDING) '95

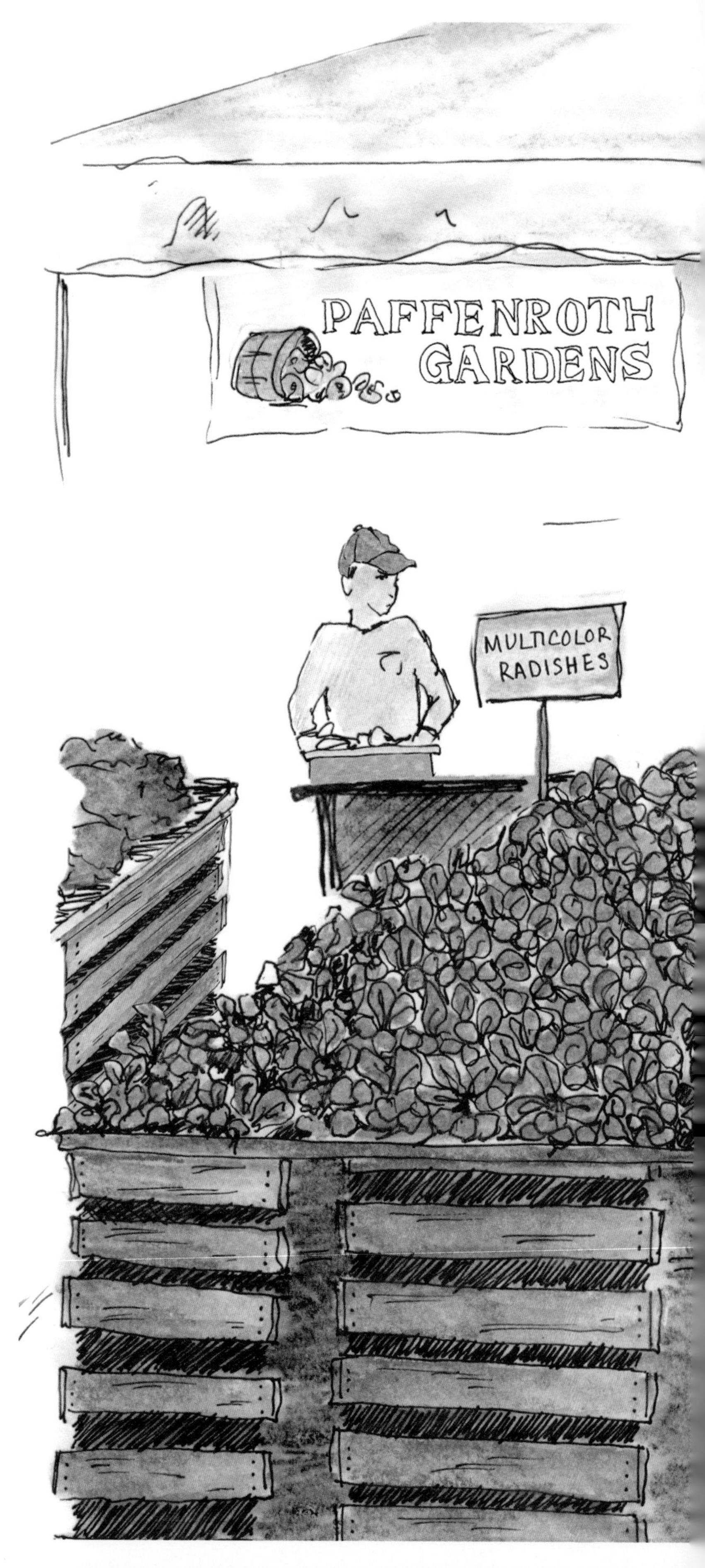
PAFFENROTH GARDENS
MULTICOLOR RADISHES

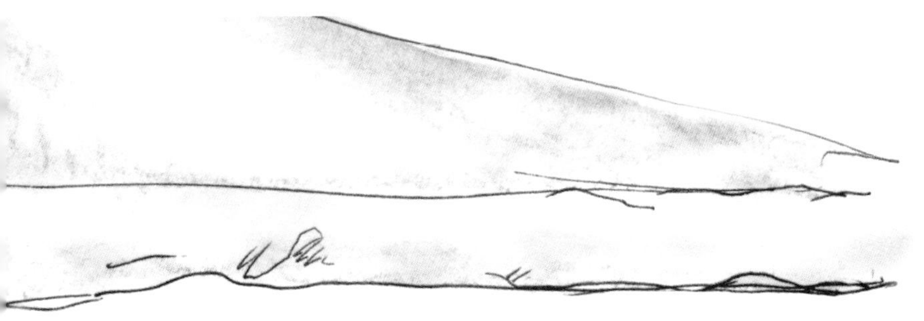

17TH STREET—UNION SQUARE FARMERS' MARKET, 5:15 P.M.

"Hell yeah!" Chalkie the cupcake baker says. ■ "That's awesome," a man in gold kicks and leopard-print leggings says. ■ "Uh, I'd better not," a more traditionally dressed man mutters. ■ "Why not?" I ask. ■ "I'm from Jersey."

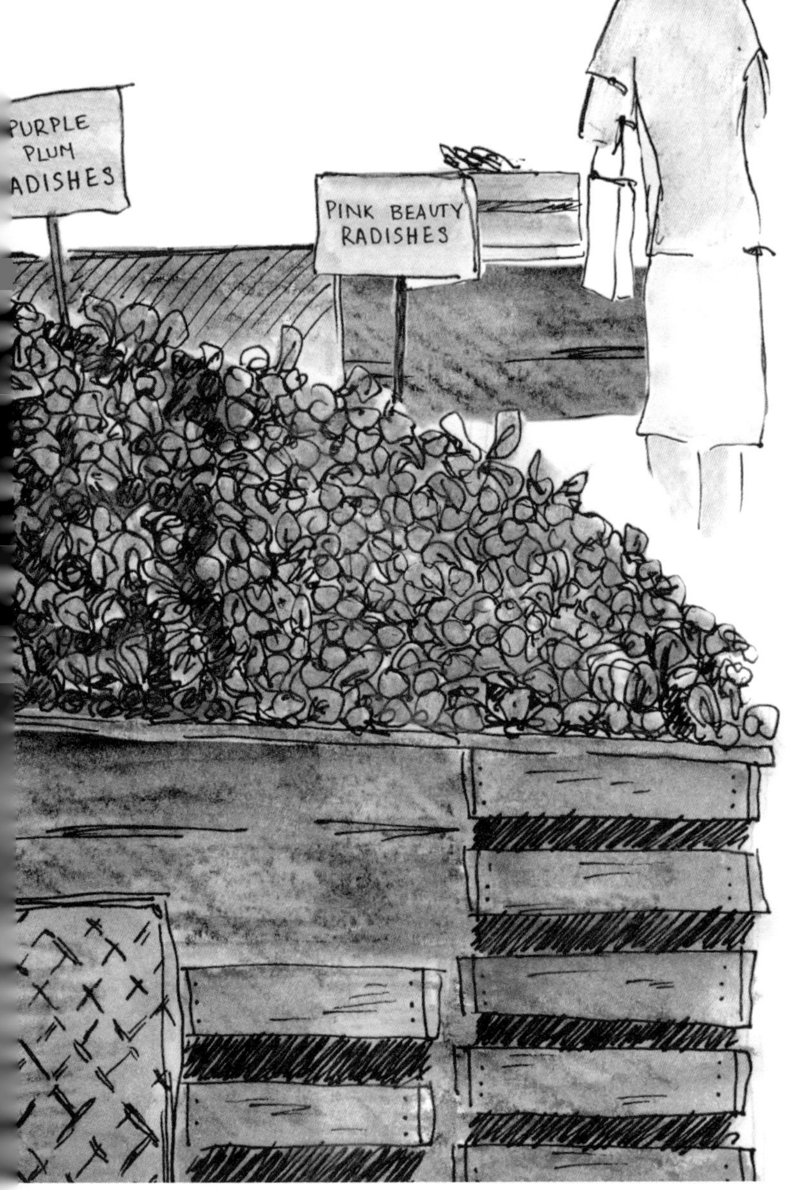

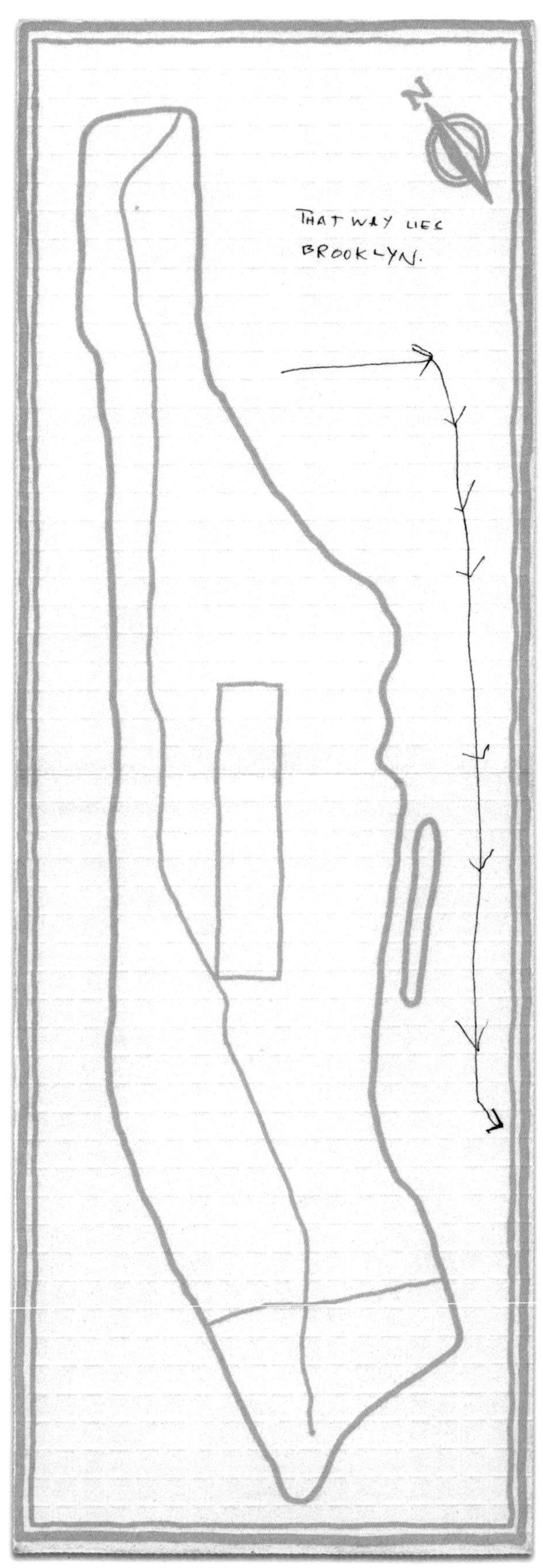
N
THAT WAY LIES
BROOKLYN.

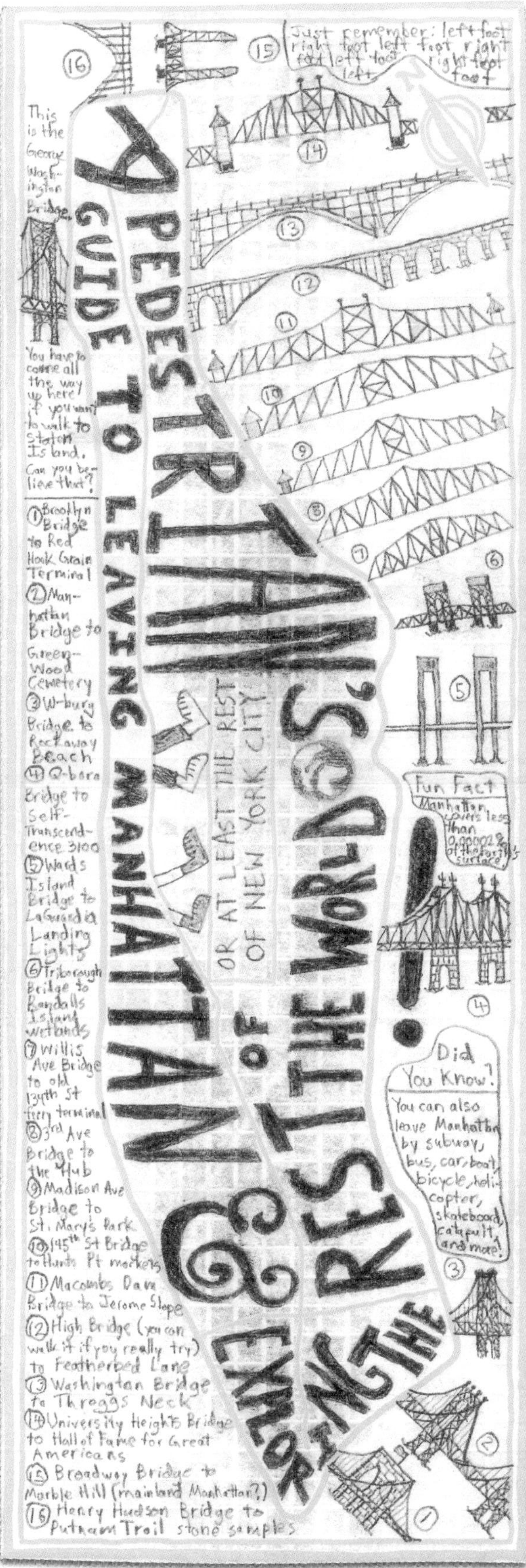
A PEDESTRIAN'S GUIDE TO LEAVING MANHATTAN & EXPLORING THE REST OF THE WORLD!
OR AT LEAST THE REST OF NEW YORK CITY
Just remember: left foot right foot left foot right foot left foot right foot left
This is the George Washington Bridge.
You have to come all the way up here if you want to walk to Staten Island. Can you believe that?
Fun Fact
Manhattan covers less than 0.00002% of the Earth's surface!
Did You Know?
You can also leave Manhattan by subway, bus, car, boat, bicycle, helicopter, skateboard, catapult, and more!
1 Brooklyn Bridge to Red Hook Grain Terminal
2 Manhattan Bridge to Green-Wood Cemetery
3 W-burg Bridge to Rockaway Beach
4 Q-boro Bridge to Self-Transcendence 3100
5 Wards Island Bridge to LaGuardia Landing Lights
6 Triborough Bridge to Randalls Island wetlands
7 Willis Ave Bridge to old 134th St ferry terminal
8 3rd Ave Bridge to the Hub
9 Madison Ave Bridge to St. Mary's Park
10 145th St Bridge to Hunts Pt markets
11 Macombs Dam Bridge to Jerome Slope
12 High Bridge (you can walk it if you really try) to Featherbed Lane
13 Washington Bridge to Throggs Neck
14 University Heights Bridge to Hall of Fame for Great Americans
15 Broadway Bridge to Marble Hill (mainland Manhattan?)
16 Henry Hudson Bridge to Putnam Trail stone samples

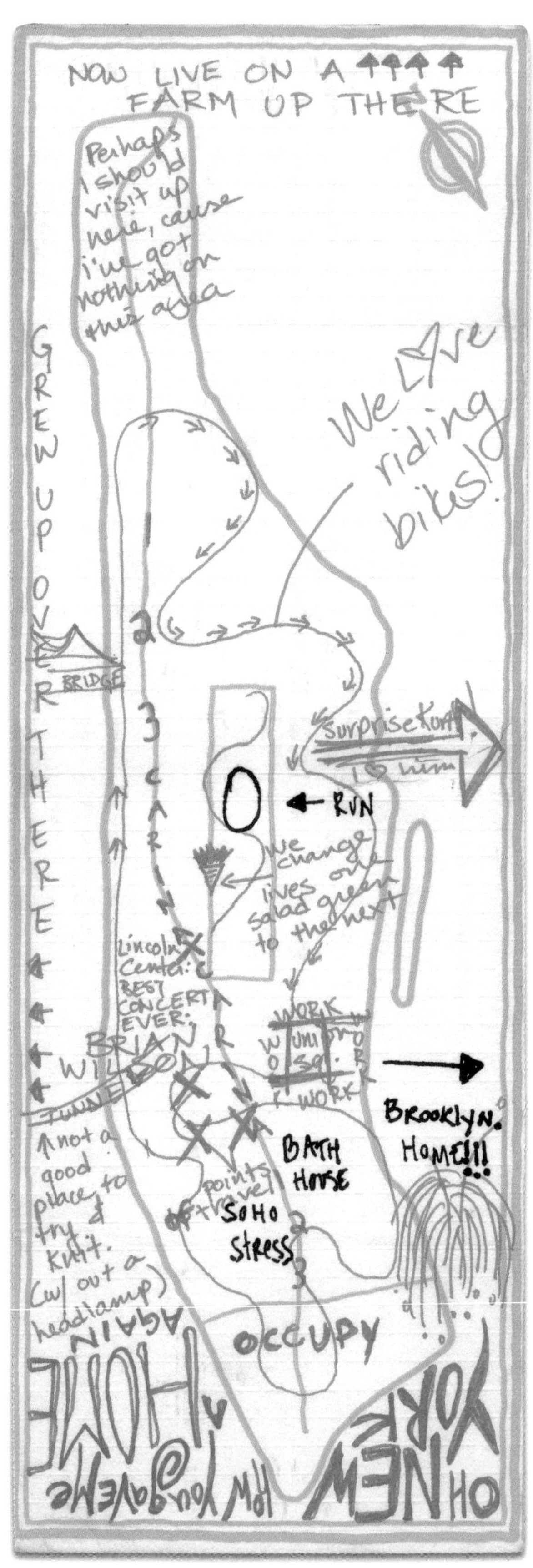
NOW LIVE ON A FARM UP THERE
Perhaps I should visit up here, cause i've got nothing on this area
GREW UP OVER THERE
We LOVE riding bikes!
BRIDGE
Surprise Kurt!
I ♥ him
RUN
We change lives one salad green to the next
Lincoln Center: BEST CONCERT EVER;
BRIAN WILSON
WORK
UNION SQ.
Brooklyn. HOME!!!
TUNNEL
not a good place to try & knit. (w/ out a headlamp)
BATH HOUSE
points of travel
SOHO STRESS
OCCUPY
OH NEW YORK
HOW YOU GAVE ME HOME AGAIN

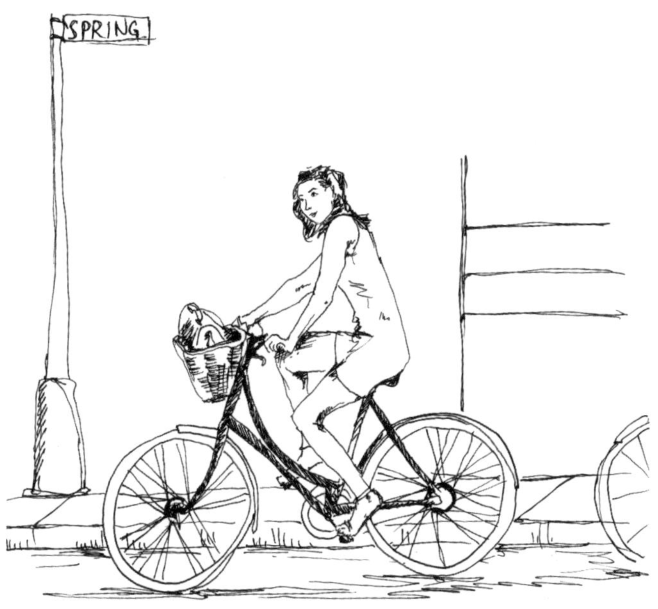

SPRING STREET, **5:46 P.M.**

Our knees ache by the time we reach SoHo, where the numbers give way to names: Prince and Spring and Mercer. It is about a quarter to six, and the easy conveyor belt of the Upper West Side has long disappeared. We are pulling ourselves along now. Fifty maps remain to be given out. ■ "Can I get a second one for my dude?" a girl in a sparkling shift dress asks, reaching out from her bike. ■ A Balthazar bartender on break hesitates for a second. "Does it have to be G-rated?" I shake my head no. He takes it. ■ At 521–523 Broadway, nestled between a Quiksilver and a Chase bank, an unassuming facade is zigzagged with a fire escape. Though you'd never guess it, the facade's brown stone was once surrounded by gorgeous white Italian marble. ■ The marble belonged to the most breathtaking hotel in New York: the St. Nicholas. When it was built in 1853, it set the standard for luxury. It spanned the block and was the first hotel to cost a million dollars to complete. Unlike the Astor, it offered central heating. The gaslight chandeliers sparkled and threw light against the frescoes. ■ But as Broadway marched north, on past Houston, this heart of luxury fell out of favor. The impeccably dressed tourists who had taken tea at the St. Nicholas wanted a hotel farther uptown, more in the center. By 1884, all of the furnishings in the hotel had been auctioned off, and the building was demolished. ■ Well, *most* of the building was demolished. That small sliver, laced with a fire escape to disguise it among the other buildings that cropped up, remains. The window carvings of 521 Broadway are the only hint of the building's extraordinary history (523's have been shaved). The ground floor of 521 is now a Puma store; 523, a Lady Footlocker.

IN 1973 ON MY FIRST TRIP TO NYC, A FRIEND TOOK ME TO McSorey's BAR. TODAY 38 YEARS LATER, STANDING ON THE STREET BY THE NEW COOPER UNION BLDG I TURNED AROUND TO SEE THE VERY SAME McSORELYS. WALKED IN WITH MY BROTHER-IN-LAW, PLACE WAS THE SAME, RIGHT DOWN TO THE FILTHY "STUFF" BEHIND THE BAR AND THE RUDE BARTENDER.

I WAS THRILLED TO SEE NOTHING HAD CHANGED

Sept. 18 · 2011

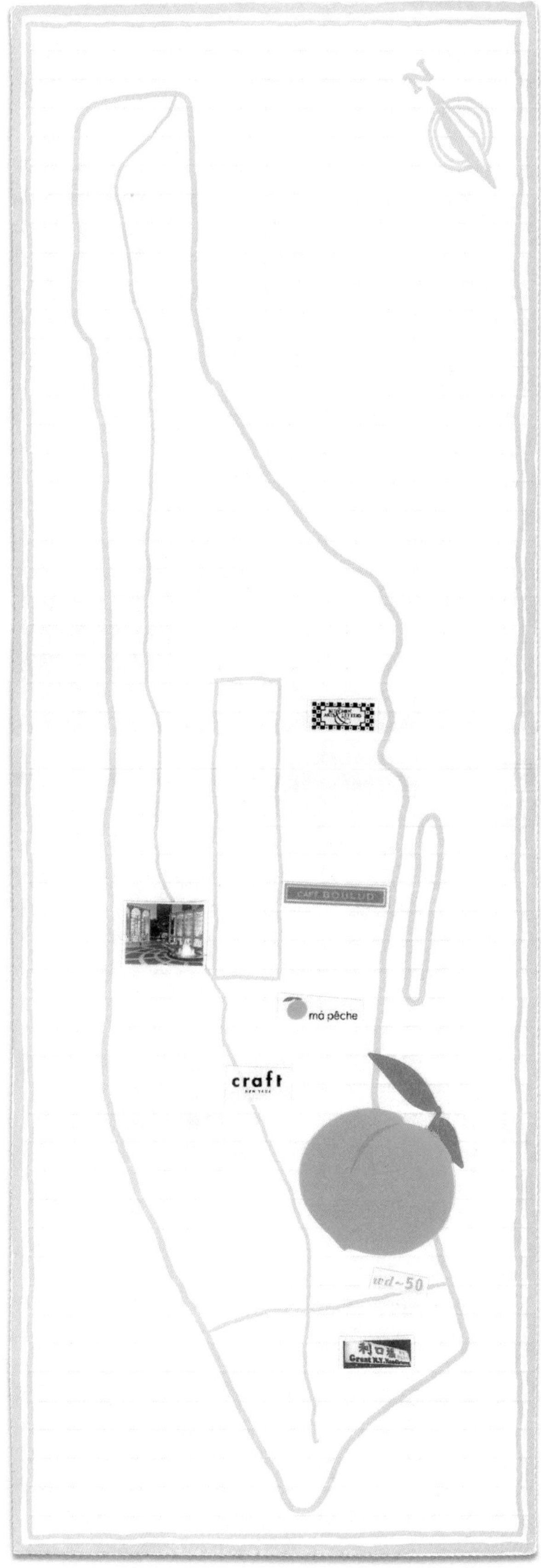

DAVID CHANG

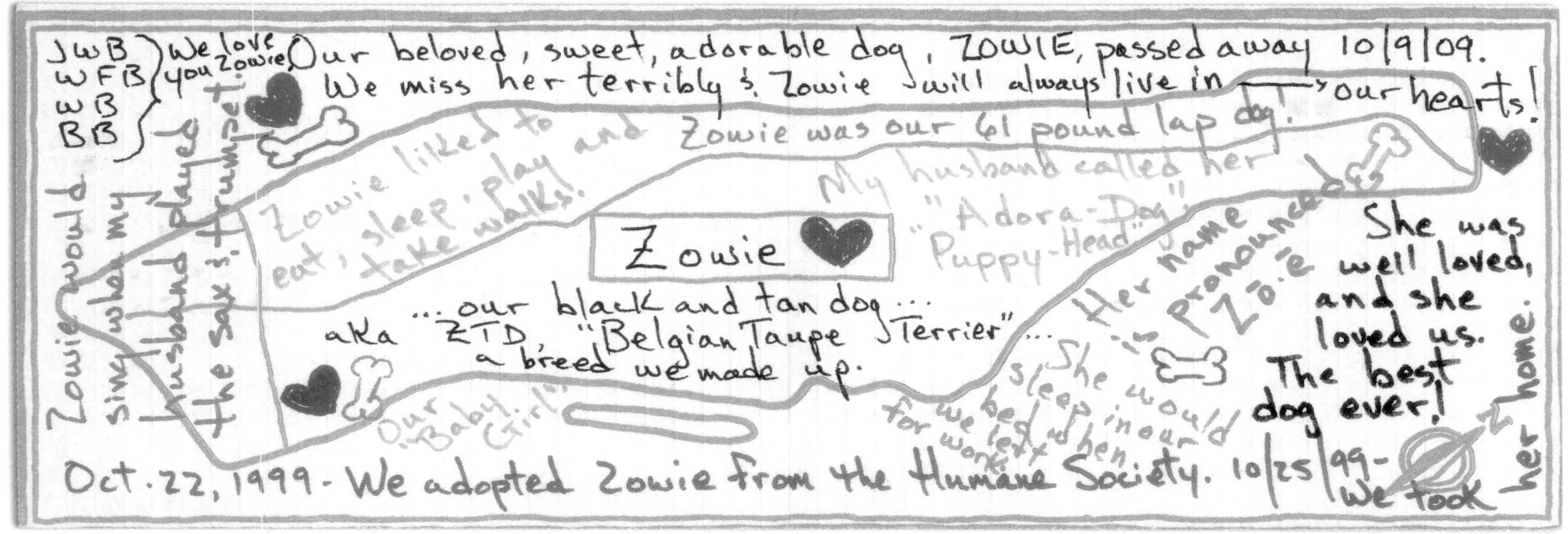
JWB
WFB
WB
BB
We love you Zowie
Our beloved, sweet, adorable dog, ZOWIE, passed away 10/9/09.
We miss her terribly & Zowie will always live in our hearts!
Zowie was our 61 pound lap dog!
Zowie liked to eat, sleep, play and take walks!
My husband called her "Adora-Dog" "Puppy-Head"
Zowie
...our black and tan dog... aka "ZTD," "Belgian Taupe Terrier"... a breed we made up.
Her name is pronounced "Zo-e"
She was well loved, and she loved us. The best dog ever!
Zowie would sing when my husband played the sax & trumpet.
Our "Baby Girl"
She would sleep in our bed when we left for work.
Oct. 22, 1999 - We adopted Zowie from the Humane Society. 10/25/99 - We took her home.

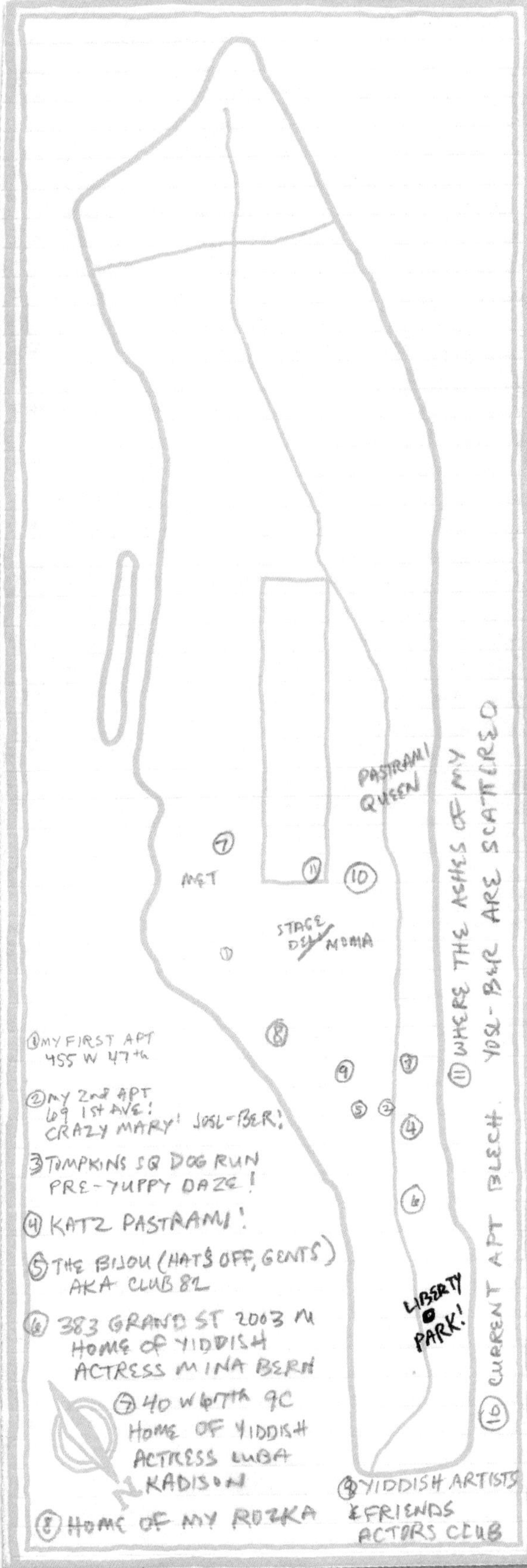
PASTRAMI QUEEN
MET
STAGE DELI
MOMA
LIBERTY PARK!
11 WHERE THE ASHES OF MY YOSL-BER ARE SCATTERED
10 CURRENT APT BLECH.
1 MY FIRST APT 455 W 47th
2 MY 2nd APT 69 1st AVE! CRAZY MARY! JOSL-BER!
3 TOMPKINS SQ DOG RUN PRE-YUPPY DAZE!
4 KATZ PASTRAMI!
5 THE BIJOU (HAT$ OFF, GENTS) AKA CLUB 82
6 383 GRAND ST 2003 M HOME OF YIDDISH ACTRESS MINA BERN
7 40 W 67th 9C HOME OF YIDDISH ACTRESS LUBA KADISON
8 HOME OF MY ROZKA
9 YIDDISH ARTISTS & FRIENDS ACTORS CLUB
N

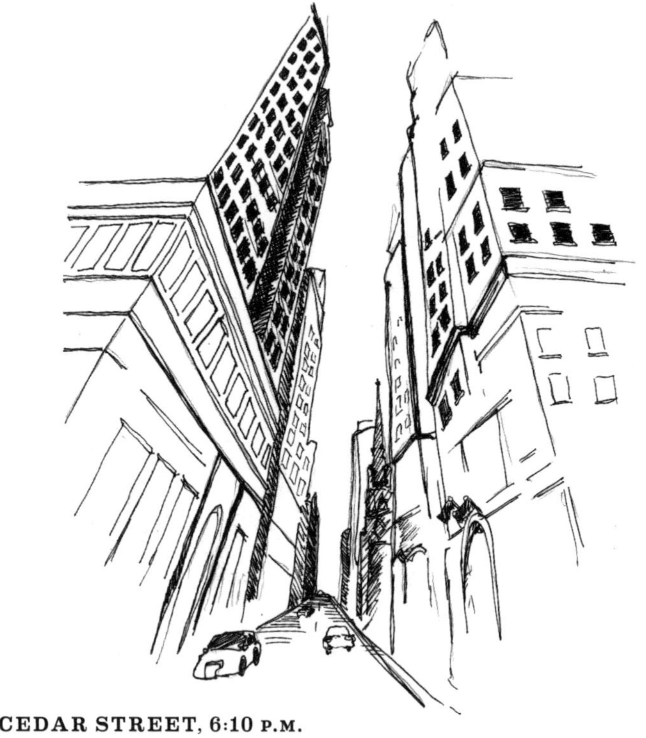

CEDAR STREET, 6:10 P.M.

The names of the streets here tell stories of New York's past: when Canal Street was a canal; Wall Street, a wall; Cedar and Pine and Beaver, resources that filled the island. Pearl Street predates British days; the name comes from when Dutch merchants gorged themselves on the abundant oysters in the waters around the city. Maiden Lane tells of the young women who washed their clothes at the brook that lay at the end of the street. ■ This is the land of New Amsterdam: Manhattan before the grid, when buildings were laid out to match the old Dutch farms back home. ■ The land just off to the west on Dey Street will, of course, be forever linked to New York history. But even before the smoke and the tears and the unfathomable loss, before the great aerialist Philippe Petit dared onlookers to dream as he walked a tightrope between the twin towers, the land was already inseparable from Manhattan's past. ■ It was waterfront. It was where the Dutch explorer Adriaen Block docked his ship, the *Tyger*, after his long transatlantic voyage in 1614. And it was where that ship burned down soon after. But Block, with the help of the native Lenape, didn't let that setback stop him. He set up camp on the island and built his new ship from the remains of the *Tyger*. ■ When Block eventually returned to the Netherlands, he brought with him a detailed new map of the territory (the first to show Manhattan as an island!) and abundant beaver pelts. With these in hand, he helped galvanize the reluctant Dutch to start colonizing New Amsterdam. ■ In 1967, Dutch cannons, possibly belonging to the *Tyger*, were recovered when the foundation of the World Trade Center was being laid. Rebirth is deep in the soil of the area.

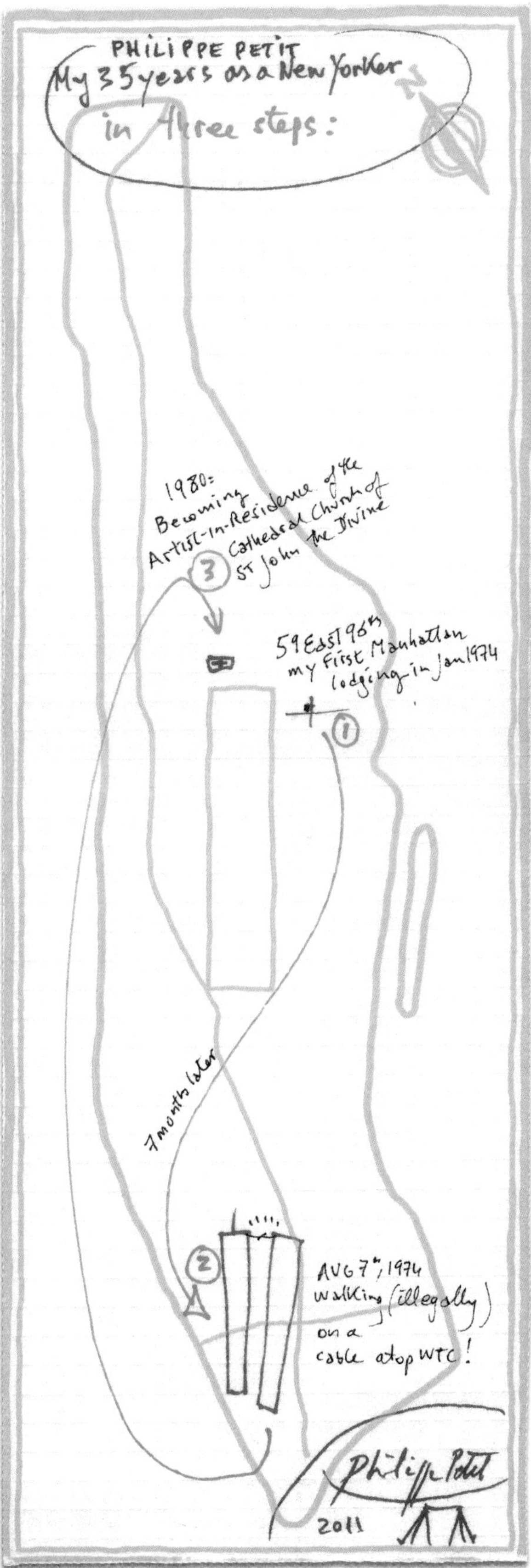
PHILIPPE PETIT
My 35 years as a New Yorker
in three steps:
1980: Becoming Artist-In-Residence of the Cathedral Church of St John the Divine
3
59 East 96th my first Manhattan lodging in Jan 1974
1
7 months later
2
AUG 7th, 1974 walking (illegally) on a cable atop WTC!
Philippe Petit
2011

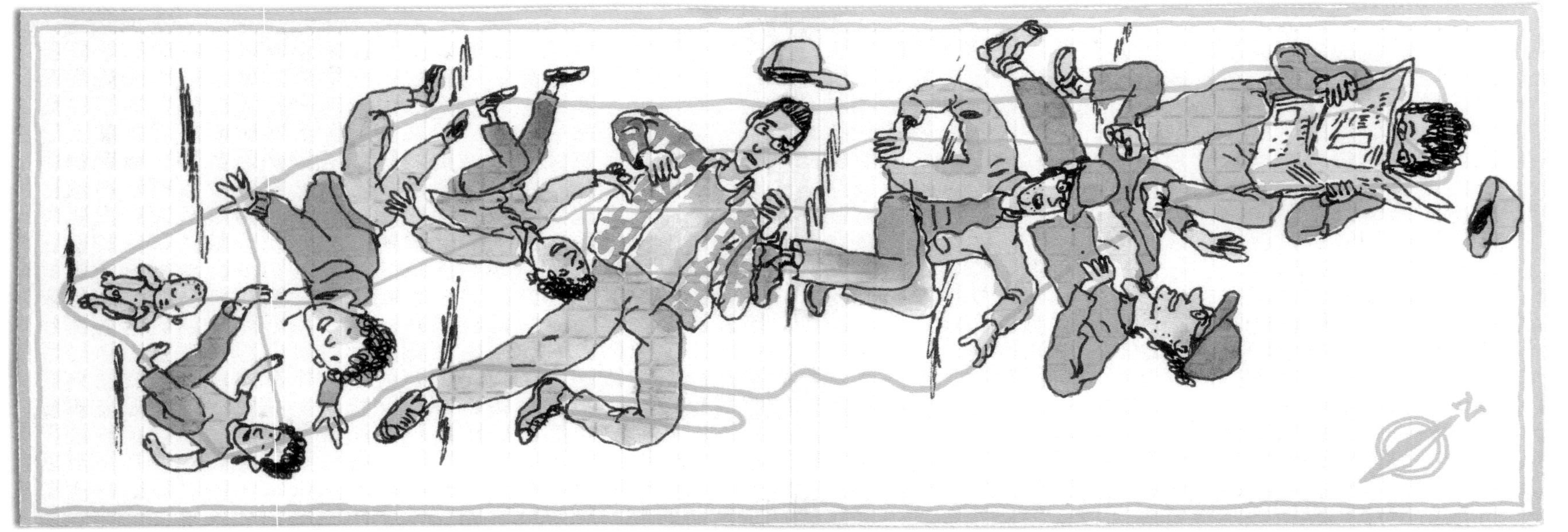

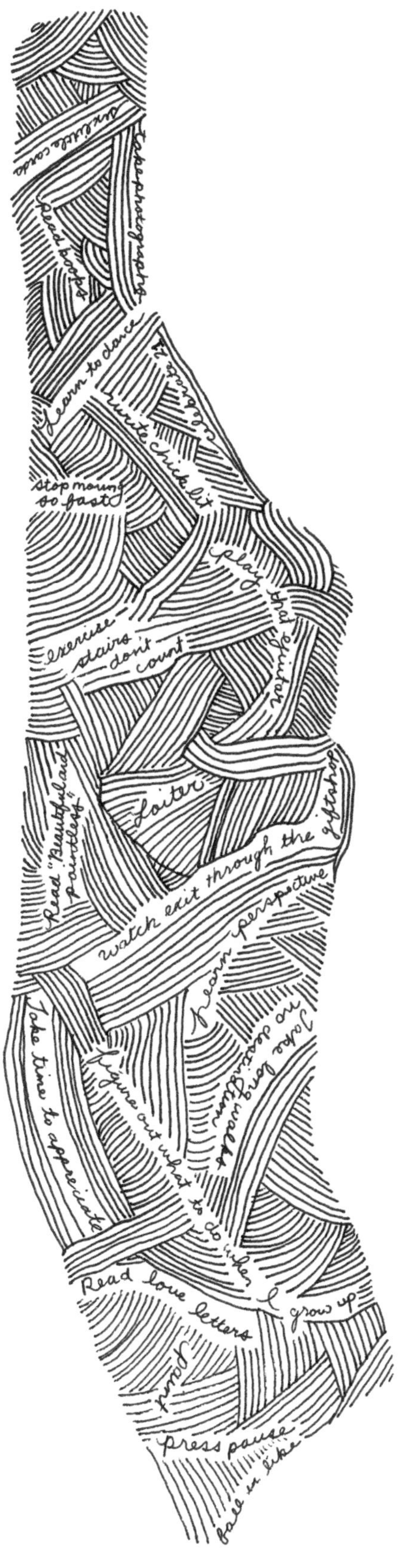
Take photographs
Read books
Learn to dance
write chick lit
stop moving so fast
play that guitar
Exercise
stairs don't count
Loiter
Read "Beautiful and Pointless"
watch exit through the giftshop
Learn perspective
Take long walks
no destination
Take time to appreciate
Figure out what to do when I grow up
Read love letters
paint
Press pause
fall in like

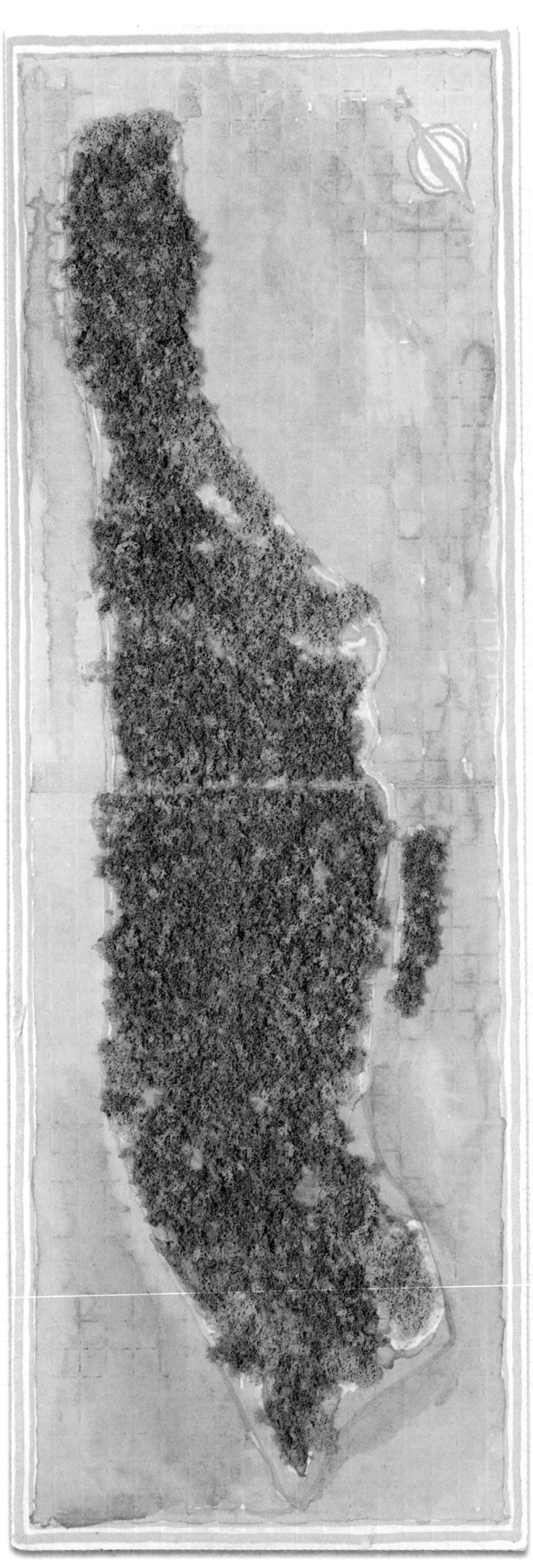

A few years ago, I started working with Eric Sanderson of the Wildlife Conservation Society on a project to reconstruct the ecosystems of Manhattan as they were when Henry Hudson first saw the island in 1609, when he sailed his ship, the Half Moon, *into the harbor and up what came to be called the Hudson River.* ■ *We gathered a lot of information by walking around Manhattan with GPS devices, looking for places—graveyards, rock outcroppings, glacier-scarred rocks in Central Park—where we could reasonably guess that the elevation had remained unchanged for 400 years. As we learned what kind of forest grew in a certain place or where the old shoreline was, we tried to see the island as it used to be.* ■ *Times Square was a freshwater marsh, but it's almost impossible to make your mind believe that while standing on the corner of 42nd and Broadway. On Minetta Lane, a tiny little street in the Village with an S curve unusual for the grid of Manhattan, we tried to imagine Minetta Brook, a trout stream that flowed down Fifth Avenue, through Washington Square Park, and southwest into the Hudson River.* ■ *Driving along the Brooklyn-Queens Expressway, I would look back at Manhattan—downtown, where the city started and the bedrock is close to the surface, and midtown, where the commuter railroads pour passengers into the city—and try to make myself see Murray Hill as a hill (with the Murrays' house on top).* ■ *In upper Manhattan, where development came later and the rocky ridges hampered construction, I can imagine, from a distance, with the trees leafed out, that I am seeing a little glimpse of what Hudson saw. In the dense tulip tree forest of Inwood Hill Park, at the northern tip of the island, there are places where I can see it almost as it was—and then I move a little, a street lamp appears, a jogger runs by, and I am back in New York City.*

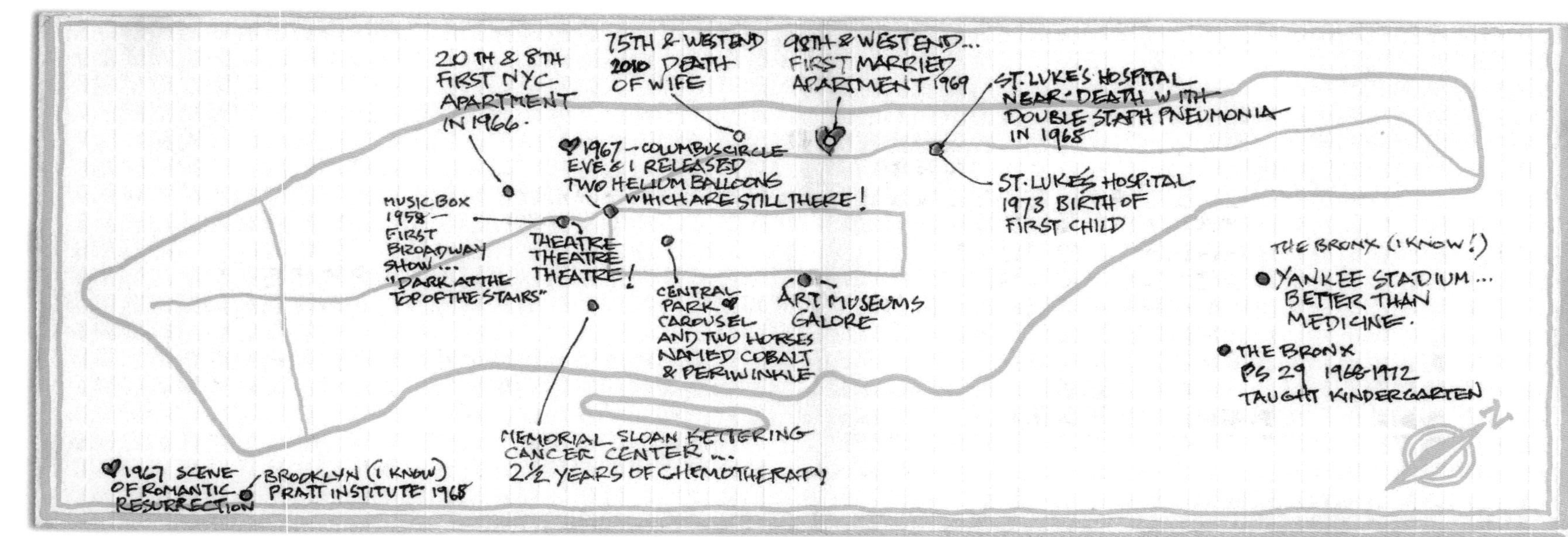
20TH & 8TH
FIRST NYC
APARTMENT
IN 1966.
75TH & WESTEND
2010 DEATH
OF WIFE
98TH & WESTEND...
FIRST MARRIED
APARTMENT 1969
ST. LUKE'S HOSPITAL
NEAR-DEATH WITH
DOUBLE STAPH PNEUMONIA
IN 1968
1967 - COLUMBUS CIRCLE
EVE & I RELEASED
TWO HELIUM BALLOONS
WHICH ARE STILL THERE!
ST. LUKE'S HOSPITAL
1973 BIRTH OF
FIRST CHILD
MUSIC BOX
1958 -
FIRST
BROADWAY
SHOW...
"DARK AT THE
TOP OF THE STAIRS"
THEATRE
THEATRE
THEATRE!
CENTRAL
PARK
CAROUSEL
AND TWO HORSES
NAMED COBALT
& PERIWINKLE
ART MUSEUMS
GALORE
THE BRONX (I KNOW!)
YANKEE STADIUM...
BETTER THAN
MEDICINE.
THE BRONX
PS 29 1968-1972
TAUGHT KINDERGARTEN
MEMORIAL SLOAN KETTERING
CANCER CENTER...
2½ YEARS OF CHEMOTHERAPY
1967 SCENE
OF ROMANTIC
RESURRECTION
BROOKLYN (I KNOW)
PRATT INSTITUTE 1968
N

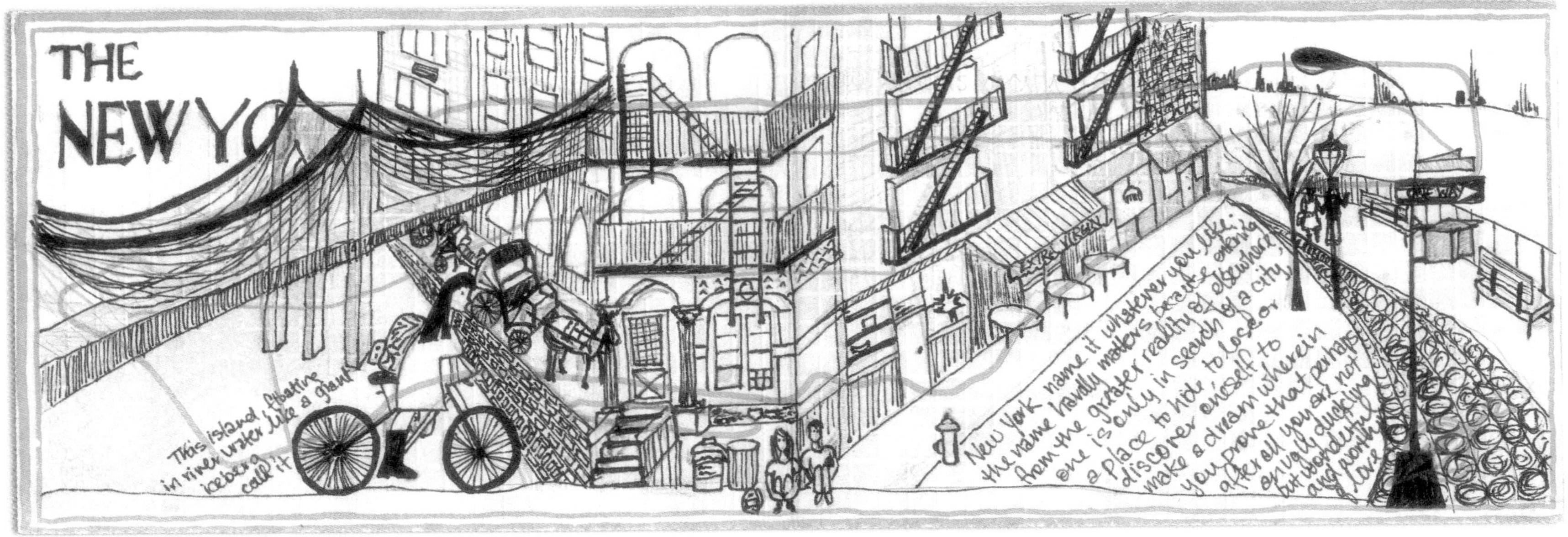
THE
NEW YO
This island floating
in river water like a giant
iceberg
call it
New York name it whatever you like;
the name hardly matters because entering
from the greater reality of elsewhere,
one is only in search of a city,
a place to hide, to lose or
discover oneself, to
make a dream wherein
you prove that perhaps
after all you are not
an ugly duckling
but wonderful
and worth
love
ONE WAY

BATTERY PARK, 6:27 P.M.

"Merci beaucoup," I say, handing the last map to a young Parisian girl sitting at the edge of Battery Park, sketching the water into her book. ■ Ama and I fall onto a bench a few down from her. I'm sore and covered in dirt—literally. I swipe my finger across my chest, and it comes up black and greasy. I am hungry and tired and lost and satisfied and exhausted. We check the time: 6:27 P.M. I mark it down. ■ It just feels so good to sit down, to sink onto a bench warmed by the sun. We stare blankly ahead, at the pedestrians and the bike riders, at the waterfront, at the confluence of the Hudson and East Rivers just beyond. ■ I try to remember why

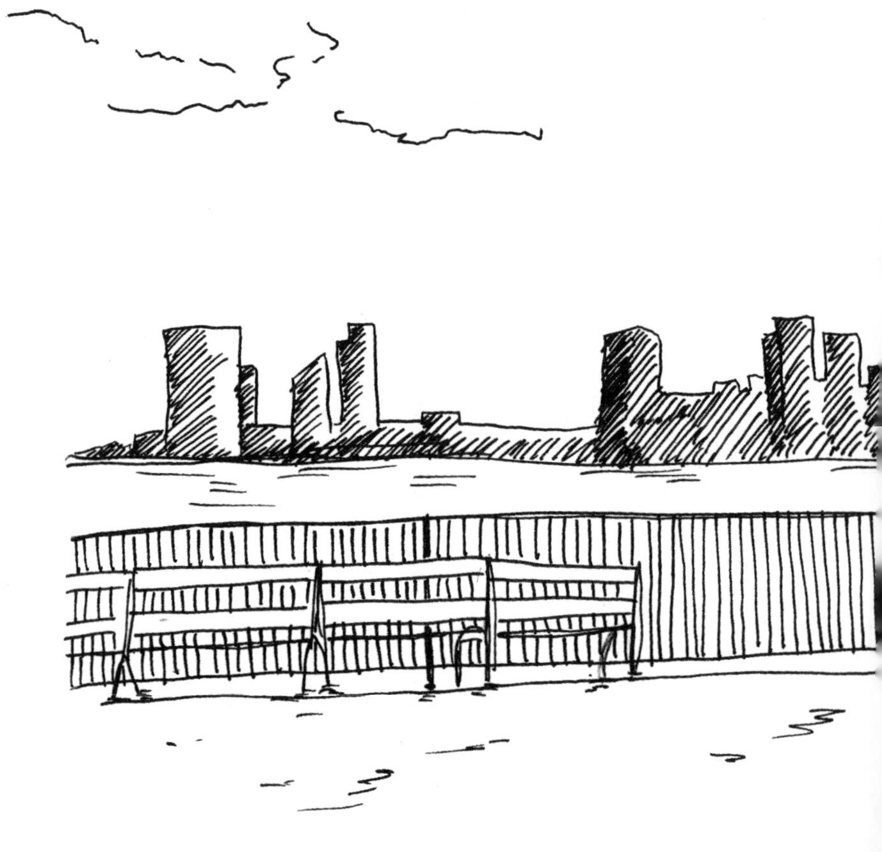

this map project meant so much to me. Why I needed to know that I could put a little bit of New York down on paper. Why I would walk 13 miles to capture just a fraction of it. Why I needed to believe that Manhattan would arrive piece by piece in my P.O. box over the next few weeks. ■ My knees ache; my shoebox of maps is empty. I've tried my best to find New York. I'm physically unable to go any farther—the street stops, and the water laces protectively around. The Statue of Liberty rises up in the distance, asserting my *hereness*. Yet the city is still essentially elsewhere. In the hearts of the people I met. In the maps they will send back. Just ahead. *There.*

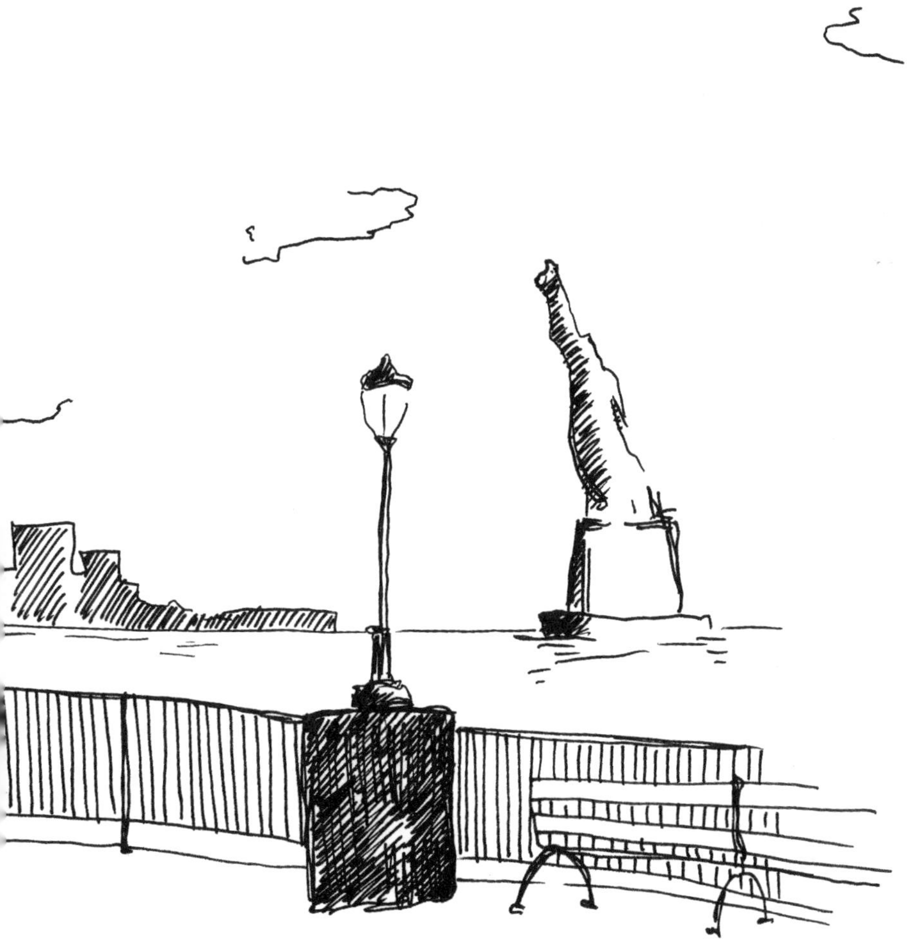

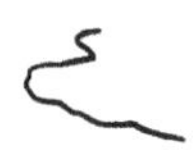

Acknowledgments

It feels almost silly to say thank you to the New Yorkers whose words, maps, and stories grace almost every inch of this book; "Thank you" doesn't even begin to cut it. You are the heart of this project. Your generosity, warmth, and willingness to share your memories made me fall in love with this city all over again. ■ My sincerest thanks also go to the contributors. I am honored that you took the time to be a part of this project; I have to pinch myself when I think about your maps being included in these pages.

Bonnie Briant, you are a saint of an illustrator, with an unbelievable talent for making straight lines look awesome. Dan Ashwood, the man behind the base map, you are a wizard. And Ama Francis, my dear adventuring companion—I would walk miles anywhere with you. Where next? ■ This book wouldn't exist without Eric Grossman, Sally Livingston, or Zachary Sifuentes. You taught me what to read, how to write, and what it means to be passionate. Thanks also to Adams House for all your support and to the Bow & Arrow Press for being my home those long, long nights of printing maps.

A huge thank-you to my family for moving to the Lower East Side generations ago and for staying put. Grandma Norma; Roberta, Gene, and Julian; the Fooses; Aunt Jeanie. Dad, thanks for being as proud of me for typing the manuscript as for writing it. And to my mother, who stayed up all night, stamping and folding each map with me: *Koala Lou.* ■ Adam Gopnik and Martha Parker, my fairy godparents, thank you for everything. ■ Meg Thompson at ETA, you are a goddess of an agent. Laura Dozier, Sarah Gifford, and the rest of the team at Abrams, thank you for turning these pages into reality. ■ I am grateful to Kenneth Jackson's *The Encyclopedia of New York City,* Hilary Ballon's *The Greatest Grid,* Paul Cohen and Robert Augustyn's *Manhattan in Maps,* and Edward Rutherford's *New York: The Novel* for helping the process of mining New York City's history for gems.

Finally—friends! Ama may have been the first person I handed out maps with, but she was certainly not the only. Lily Erlinger,

Liz Livingstone, Erin Miles, Brian Polk, Anna Sakellariadis—thank you, and apologize again to your feet on my behalf. ■ Thanks also to Gracia Angulo, Alex Arzoumanov, Noel Barlow, and Sarah Berlow; my eagle eyes: Ben Burns and Pat Chesnut; Abi Crutchfield, Charlie "Cheeks" Damga, Svetlana Dotsenko, Mike Einziger, Emmie Francis, Tony Hernandez, Laurence Holland, Anna Kamerow, Victor Kerlow, Russ Lebo, Joyce Lee, Ben Naddaff-Hafrey, Hamida Owusu, Zanda Panda, Elsa Paparemborde, Michael Pietsch, Zander Rafael, Alissa Schapiro, Katie Schick, Kevin Seitz, David Smith, Abby Suckle, Grace Sun, Ben Tarnoff, Alex and Jules Terrien, Parker VanValkenburgh, Hugo Van Vuuren, Larissa Zhou, and, of course, Gideon Wald. You urged me to start, encouraged me to continue, and worked your magic to the end.

Last, but not least: Harvard College Research Program, thanks for the stamps.

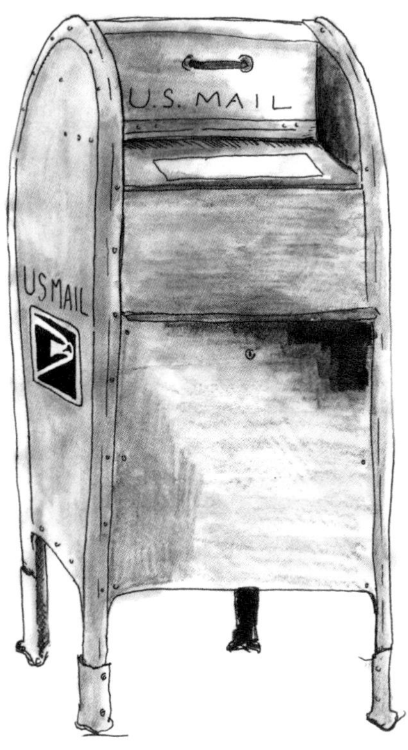

About the Contributors

ERIC ASIMOV is the chief wine critic of the *New York Times* and the author of *How to Love Wine: A Memoir and Manifesto* (William Morrow, 2012).

MARKLEY BOYER is the illustrator of *Mannahatta: A Natural History of New York* (Abrams, 2009), a book that reconstructs Manhattan as Henry Hudson saw it in 1609. Boyer is an expert on landscape visualization.

DAVID CHANG is the chef and owner of the Momofuku restaurants, with locations in New York City, Sydney, Australia, and soon in Toronto, Canada. The winner of three James Beard Foundation awards, he was named one of *Time*'s 100, *GQ* Man of the Year, and one of "the most influential people of the 21st century" by *Esquire*. He is also the cocreator and editor of *Lucky Peach*, a quarterly journal of food and writing published by McSweeney's.

RANDY COHEN is a writer and humorist. He was the original writer of The Ethicist for the *New York Times*. Before that, he was an Emmy Award–winning writer for *Late Night with David Letterman*. He and Nigel Holmes once made a literary map of Manhattan for the *Times*, which documented "where imaginary New Yorkers lived, worked, played, drank, walked, and looked at ducks."

KATE CORDES is the head of the Lionel Pincus and Princess Firyal Map Division at the New York Public Library.

EUGENE DRUCKER is a founding member of the Emerson String Quartet, with which he has won nine Grammys and the Avery Fisher Prize. He is also the author of the novel *The Savior*, published by Simon & Schuster. He lives on the Upper West Side with his wife, cellist Roberta Cooper, and their son, Julian.

HARVEY FIERSTEIN is the four-time Tony Award–winning author of *Torch Song Trilogy*, *La Cage aux Folles*, *Newsies*, and *The Sissy Duckling*. As a stage actor, he's starred in *Hairspray*, *Fiddler on the Roof*, and *Torch Song Trilogy*, among others. His TV and film appearances include *Mrs. Doubtfire*, *Independence Day*, *The Good Wife*, and an Emmy-nominated role in *Cheers*.

LIANA FINCK is a poet and artist. As a 2010–2012 Six Points Fellow, she wrote and illustrated a graphic novel based on the Bintel Brief, the *Jewish Daily Forward*'s advice column that helped generations of Yiddish immigrants adjust to life in America.

CAIO FONSECA, an American painter, was born and raised in Manhattan's West Village. His works are held in numerous private and public collections, including the Met, MoMA, and the Whitney.

MALCOLM GLADWELL is a staff writer for the *New Yorker* and the author of four *New York Times* number-one bestsellers, including, most recently, *What the Dog Saw*. He was born in England, grew up in Canada, lives in Manhattan, and keeps threatening to move to Williamsburg.

RICHARD GOODMAN is the author of four nonfiction books, including *A New York Memoir*. He is an assistant professor of English at the University of New Orleans.

ADAM GOPNIK is a three-time National Magazine Award winner, the recipient of the George Polk Award for Magazine Reporting, and the author of multiple national bestsellers. He has been a staff writer for the *New Yorker* since 1986, contributing pieces spanning art and baseball, Paris and politics. He currently lives in New York with his wife and two children.

After walking more than 3,000 miles across the United States in 2010, **MATT GREEN,** a former civil engineer, set his sights on a three-year, 8,000-mile quest to walk every block in New York City.

ERIC GROSSMAN, the assistant principal of English at Stuyvesant High School in Manhattan, lives in Brooklyn with his wife and two children. He is the reason I read Italo Calvino's *Invisible Cities* and is therefore a major reason this book exists.

The name **KATHARINE HARMON** is practically synonymous with creative cartography. She is the author of *The Map as Art* and *You Are Here: Personal Geographies and Other Maps of the Imagination*.

ALLEN M. HART is a painter whose work is in the permanent collections of the University of Massachusetts, the Butler Institute of American Art, and the Children's Aid Society. The Little Red Lighthouse, depicted in his map, is his fondest memory of growing up in Washington Heights in the 1930s.

BRIAN HUGHES is the director of protective services at the Intrepid Sea, Air and Space Museum. He has also worked at the American Museum of Natural History, served in the US Army, and was a lieutenant with the New York Police Department for more than twenty years. He responded to the call on September 11, 2001, and worked on recovery at the site until June 2002.

New Yorker staff writer **PATRICIA MARX** has lived in Manhattan for twenty-two years and is still annoyed with Broadway for running on a diagonal.

VAHRAM MURATYAN is a French graphic artist whose blog *Paris versus New York* is a collection of pithy visual comparisons of the two iconic cities. (Baguette vs. Bagel; Quasimodo vs. King Kong; Godard vs. Woody.) The book by the same name was published in 2012.

YOKO ONO is a visual artist, musician, and activist. Her contribution to the Central Park Conservancy in the 1980s provided for the redesign and restoration of the Strawberry Fields memorial, a tribute to her late husband, John Lennon. She still lives in the Dakota, the building that looks out onto Strawberry Fields.

Besides having stretched a steel cable without permission between the towers of the World Trade Center in New York City, high-wire artist **PHILIPPE PETIT** writes, draws, gives lectures on creativity and motivation, performs close-up magic, practices lock-picking and 18th century timber framing, plays chess, and was recently sighted bullfighting in Peru. Also he has been arrested over 500 times... for street juggling!

GREGORY SERBE is the president of Lebenthal Asset Management. The parent company, Lebenthal & Co., was among the first to sell municipal bonds to individual investors when it opened at 120 Broadway in 1925.

NEIL DEGRASSE TYSON is an astrophysicist and the director of the Hayden Planetarium at the American Museum of Natural History. He was born and raised in New York City. Dr. Tyson coined the term Manhattanhenge to describe a semiannual event that occurs when the setting sun aligns precisely with the east-west line of the Manhattan grid and illuminates the steel-and-glass buildings with a fire-bright intensity.

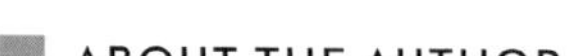

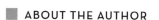

ABOUT THE AUTHOR

Becky Cooper was raised in Queens but grew up in Manhattan at Stuyvesant High School. In 2010, she graduated Phi Beta Kappa from Harvard University, where she studied Comparative Literature and Mind, Brain, and Behavior. The recipient of the Thomas T. Hoopes Prize for her senior thesis on David Foster Wallace, she is often lost, usually wandering, and always looking for the next adventure.

ABOUT THE ILLUSTRATOR

Bonnie Briant is a designer and photographer who was raised in Rhode Island and lives in New York City, where she received her BFA from New York University's Tisch School of the Arts. Her photographs and designs have been featured in magazines and exhibitions internationally. In sixth grade she advanced to the state level of the National Geography Bee.

ABOUT THE PROJECT

Map Your Memories is an ongoing collaborative art project that asks people to fill in blank maps of a city with what makes the place special to them. Becky Cooper created the project in 2007 with outlines of Manhattan and has since expanded it to Cambridge, Massachusetts, and Portland, Maine. It has been featured in the *Wall Street Journal* and *Time Out New York* and in gallery shows in New York and Boston. Maps continue to be posted on www.mapyourmemories.com.

Cut here

Fold

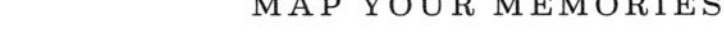

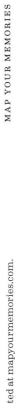

■ 1. Cut along dotted lines. ■ 2. Fill in your map. ■ 3. Fold the card in half and tape it closed.
■ 4. Add a stamp and mail it in. Your map may be posted at mapyourmemories.com.

MAP YOUR MEMORIES

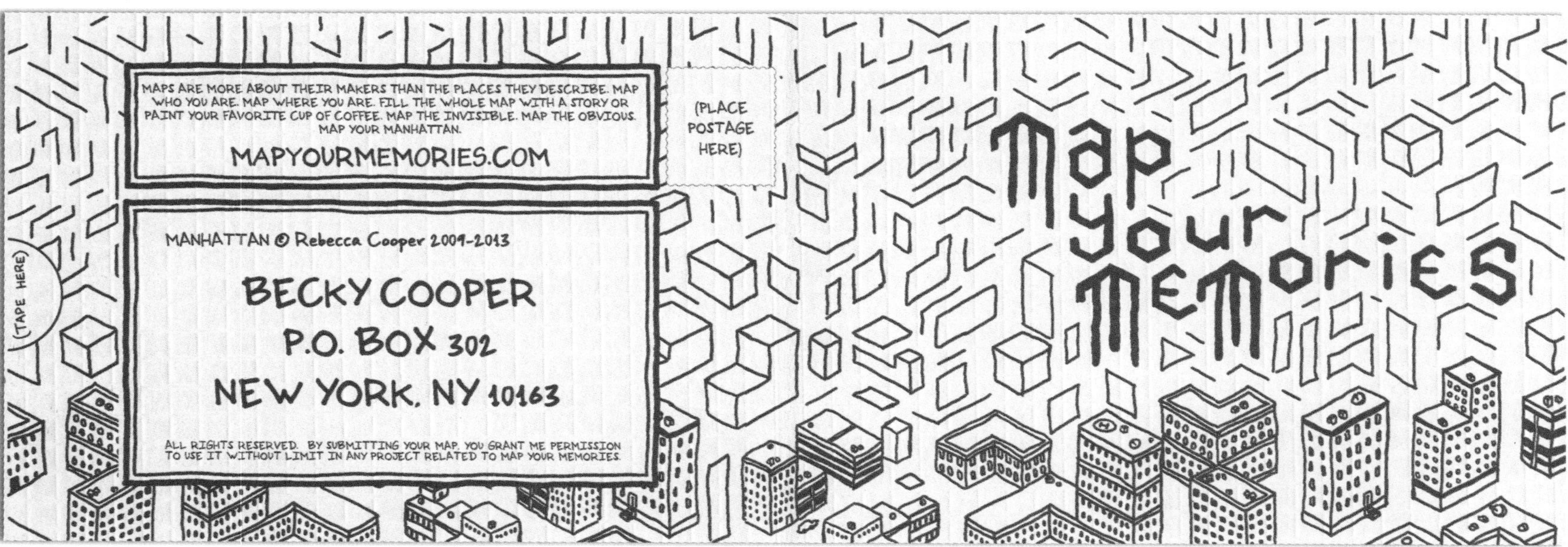
MAPS ARE MORE ABOUT THEIR MAKERS THAN THE PLACES THEY DESCRIBE. MAP WHO YOU ARE. MAP WHERE YOU ARE. FILL THE WHOLE MAP WITH A STORY OR PAINT YOUR FAVORITE CUP OF COFFEE. MAP THE INVISIBLE. MAP THE OBVIOUS. MAP YOUR MANHATTAN.
MAPYOURMEMORIES.COM
(PLACE POSTAGE HERE)
Map your Memories
MANHATTAN © Rebecca Cooper 2009-2013
BECKY COOPER
P.O. BOX 302
NEW YORK, NY 10163
ALL RIGHTS RESERVED. BY SUBMITTING YOUR MAP, YOU GRANT ME PERMISSION TO USE IT WITHOUT LIMIT IN ANY PROJECT RELATED TO MAP YOUR MEMORIES.
(TAPE HERE)